D0065147

Rescue Road

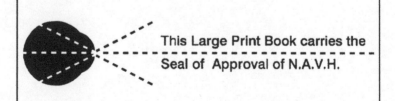

RESCUE ROAD

ONE MAN, THIRTY THOUSAND DOGS, AND A MILLION MILES ON THE LAST HOPE HIGHWAY

PETER ZHEUTLIN

THORNDIKE PRESS
A part of Gale, Cengage Learning

GALE
CENGAGE Learning·

Farmington Hills, Mich • San Francisco • New York • Waterville, Maine
Meriden, Conn • Mason, Ohio • Chicago

Thorndike Press® Large Print Inspirational.
The text of this Large Print edition is unabridged.
Other aspects of the book may vary from the original edition.
Set in 16 pt. Plantin.

LIBRARY OF CONGRESS CATALOGING-IN-PUBLICATION DATA

Zheutlin, Peter, author.
    Rescue road : one man, thirty thousand dogs and a million miles on the last hope highway / by Peter Zheutlin. — Large print edition.
        pages cm. — (Thorndike Press large print inspirational)
        ISBN 978-1-4104-8542-7 (hardcover) — ISBN 1-4104-8542-0 (hardcover)
        1. Dog rescue. 2. Animal welfare. I. Title.
HV4746.Z44 2016
636.7'0832092—dc23
[B]   2015031719

Published in 2016 by arrangement with Sourcebooks, Inc.

Printed in Mexico
1 2 3 4 5 6 7 20 19 18 17 16

For my brother, Michael, with love.

CONTENTS

INTRODUCTION

In 2012 the Berlin Wall fell. Okay, not *that* Berlin Wall; the Germans knocked theirs down in 1989. I'm talking about my own wall of opposition to having a dog in the family. That Berlin Wall survived the end of the Cold War by more than twenty years. But when it fell, I fell hard for a dog named Albie.

For years my wife, Judy, and sons, Danny and Noah, had pleaded with me to consider adopting a dog. I held them at bay with turtles, hamsters, fish, and eventually a cockatiel named Houdini whose messy cage I cleaned every week for ten years and who I secretly hoped would live up to his namesake and escape all on his own. But I insisted: no dog. *Too much work. Too much responsibility. You can't travel with a dog. I have allergies. The dog will shed everywhere. I'll be the one getting up in the wee hours of those subfreezing February mornings risking*

life and limb on sheets of ice so the dog can poop. Even though I had a dog growing up, sorry, not going to happen. I used every excuse in the book. Then, I ran out of excuses.

We've had Albie, a yellow Lab mix, for three years now, and he's the love of my life, the apple of my eye, my best friend, and every other trite cliché you can think of. I'm sixty-one, and we're going to grow old together. Chances are I will outlive him and I'm already dreading the day we part. Believe me, when I used to hear people talk this way about their dogs, I thought they were slightly daft or had difficulty forming relationships with other people. Now I get it. Completely. I was totally unprepared for the depth of my feelings for this beautiful, trusting, loving creature.

I can trace my change of heart to the weekend we took care of Reilly, our friends' black Lab, while they were away. Reilly nudged me in the right direction. I told Judy we could look around, but I wasn't ready to commit. Around the same time, a guy in Judy's yoga class brought his dog, Tige, to class. He told her he'd adopted her through Labs4rescue, a Connecticut-based organization that matches families, primarily in the Northeast, with Labs rescued mainly from high-kill shelters in the South.[1] Tige, he said, was absolutely the best dog he'd ever had. Judy started looking at pictures and videos online of dogs available through Labs4rescue and filled out an application.

When Judy first said the words "rescue dog," I imagined a Saint Bernard with a small barrel of whiskey under its chin, roaming the Alps in search of avalanche survivors. I was completely ignorant. When she explained, my head — like many people's — filled with pre-conceived notions about shelter, or rescue dogs. I assumed they were damaged goods, behaviorally unpredictable,

1. Founded in 2002, Labs4rescue has helped more than 12,000 Labs and Lab mixes find homes.

susceptible to health problems, and maybe even slightly dangerous. Nothing, I have since learned, could be further from the truth. But at the time I was especially uncertain about adopting a rescue dog.[2] Nor was I aware of the enormous number of beautiful, deserving dogs desperately in need of homes, especially in the South.

A few weeks later, my older son, Danny (then twenty-one), and I took an outdoor grilling class taught by our friend Chef Chris Schlesinger. He brought along his new black Lab, Sal, who was mellow and unobtrusive. A little jolt of envy passed through me, and not just because Chris has talents at the grill I can only dream of. It

2. For anyone who has a dog or is thinking of getting one (rescue or not), I highly recommend reading *Inside of a Dog: What Dogs See, Smell, and Know* by Alexandra Horowitz, a canine cognition expert who teaches psychology at Barnard College, Columbia University. For those wary of adopting rescue dogs because of their often uncertain pedigree, Professor Horowitz says, "The myth that a shelter dog, especially a mixed breed dog, will be less good or less reliable than a purchased dog is not just wrong, it is entirely backward: mixed breeds are healthier, less anxious, and live longer than purebreds."

was his bond with Sal. The dog adored him and vice versa. *That,* I thought, *is a beautiful thing.*

By the time I came home that evening, my reticence had turned into determination. I said to Judy, "Let's get a dog."

We quickly learned that the rescue movement was much bigger than we imagined — once we started asking it seemed everyone we ran into with a dog had a "rescue" — and that the matching of dogs and families largely takes place online. The Internet has played a huge role in the growth of the canine rescue movement, especially in pairing and moving thousands of abused, abandoned, and neglected dogs from the South to forever homes in the North. (We'll come to the question of why there are so many southern dogs later.) Sites such as Petfinder .com, used by many rescue groups including Labs4rescue, are the Match.coms of the canine world. On these websites, eager adoptive families can peruse pictures of countless dogs waiting for their forever homes, read what their temporary caregivers have to say about them, learn what is known about their previous lives — which is usually little — and, in some cases, watch a short video showing the dog interacting with people, fetching a ball, or just generally looking absolutely adorable.

And this is exactly what we did once our Cold War over canines finally ended. When Judy came across Albie online, she thought she'd met the One. In the short video, his eyes were soulful, his tail was always wagging, and he seemed to be pleading for someone to love him. She hurried into my office with her laptop so I could see for myself. Somewhere between two and three years old, he'd been found wandering, frightened and alone, by a country road in central Louisiana. Now, he was in a high-kill shelter in Alexandria, Louisiana.

My heart also jumped as I watched Albie, confined in a small, fenced grassy area, chase a ball and trot back proudly to someone who was off camera, his tail wagging a mile a minute. He was so earnest, so eager to please, and so obviously sweet tempered. Thirty short seconds and I could already feel myself attaching to this lovable creature twelve hundred miles away. Even though I knew it was a huge leap of faith to commit to a dog you only know from watching a video (after all, the video isn't going to show the dog at his worst, just his best), I was smitten.

Judy and I immediately emailed Albie's

Labs4rescue adoption coordinator, Keri Bullock Toth of the Humane Society of Central Louisiana (who, as you'll see in later chapters, is one of the true unsung heroes of the rescue movement), and asked a few questions to reassure ourselves that Albie was as he appeared in the video. "He has manners," she replied and verified everything was as it seemed. Thus assured, we set the process in motion, which included a home visit by a local Labs4rescue volunteer in Massachusetts to ensure we were as responsible as we appeared as well. Reputable rescue groups go to great lengths to try and assure successful adoptions. Some of these dogs have been the victims of unspeakable neglect or abuse; many have just been the victims of plain old bad luck. When they place a dog, unless it's a temporary foster to get them to a safe place, they are truly looking for a forever home. That's why they also carefully screen the dogs for adoptability and prepare them for their new lives; they assess temperament, and they do everything they can to make sure the dogs are healthy, current on all immunizations and other preventatives, and, importantly, spayed or neutered.

Once the preliminaries were out of the way, Albie was ours. Now the only question was when Keri could find a space on the transport that Labs4rescue relies on to bring many of their dogs north from Louisiana.

The wait was excruciating. Albie, of course, had no idea he was going anywhere or that he had a forever family already in love and waiting for him. But we couldn't wait a minute longer to open our home to Albie. We kept watching the thirty-second video over and over, our attachment growing each time, until we caught a break a few days later. There was room for one more dog on that week's transport.

Most people who do canine rescue work will move heaven and earth to save a single dog. Keri drove more than two hours from her home in the wee hours of the morning to Lafayette, Louisiana, to meet a man named Greg Mahle ("May-lee"), who runs an organization called Rescue Road Trips, and get Albie onto his truck. (At the time, Greg wasn't picking up dogs in Alexandria, where Keri is based.) When Keri told me this, the whole operation reminded me of that image of the last helicopter out of Saigon before South Vietnam fell to the North. All I could do was admire and be grateful for her extraordinary effort to get our beloved Albie to us.

I didn't know Greg's name then, nor had I heard of his transport service. In fact, I had no concept of what "transport" was or how it worked. And I definitely had no clue how much Greg Mahle would change my life. I only knew that Albie would arrive in three days and would have to spend forty-eight hours in quarantine at a facility a couple of towns over from ours before we could pick him up.[3]

Knowing Albie was safely on board, Judy started following Greg's progress online. Greg documents every trip he makes on Facebook, posting pictures and short updates about where he is and how the dogs are faring. On the second day, she came running into my office again and practically dumped her open laptop onto my desk. "Look! It's Albie!" she exclaimed.

There, on Greg's Rescue Road Trips Facebook page was a picture of Albie, a little red kerchief around his neck, sitting upright with his paws in Greg's hands, his head turned directly toward the camera. Under

3. Some states, including Massachusetts, require imported rescue dogs to be quarantined. The practice is controversial, however, as many believe it is unnecessary and ineffective.

the picture, Greg had written this:

"The stress of everything got to be a little much. Had to breathe. Labs4rescue Albie suggested he and I take a walk and try to relax me a bit. As we were walking, he told me how excited for me he was. I told him how excited for him I was. We hugged and then sat and talked a while longer. Then he suggested we hop back in the truck and get this journey finished up, because we both have our 'happily ever afters' waiting for us at the end of this run. And neither of us wants to be late.

"We just crossed the Mason–Dixon. We are in the North. I hope you are as excited as we are. It won't be long now. Get Ready! The wait is almost over. We are almost home."

Judy and I both teared up. He was now not just legally ours but *ours* — to love and protect and provide for.

When the wait ended at last, Judy and Noah drove to the quarantine facility in nearby Medfield, Massachusetts, to bring Albie home. It seemed to them as though he had never ridden in a car before. He didn't seem to know how to get in and stood nervously the entire ride home. When they pulled up in front of our house, he jumped out, but it was clear he had no idea he had reached his forever home and his forever people. He was excited but confused, running a few steps this way, then that, unsure of what would happen next. He didn't seem afraid, just a bit like an unguided missile. We were simply strangers to him, and he wasn't sure whether to come in the house with us or wander around the yard, sniffing his surroundings.

For two weeks, we couldn't coax Albie upstairs at nighttime. We surmised he'd never lived in a house with stairs, but really, we had no idea what his previous life had been. We could only speculate. He slept under the coffee table in the living room. When he finally screwed up enough courage to come upstairs (to this day he's never descended the stairs to the basement), he slept under our bed for weeks. Something about being under furniture made him feel secure.

Then he made what I call his leap of faith. My Berlin Wall had fallen, but I had one last red line: no dogs sleeping in bed with us. But one day, I came upstairs at bedtime, and there was Albie in our bed, curled up, his head resting on the pillow. He looked at me plaintively, clearly unsure if this was acceptable and perhaps expecting to be reprimanded. But as we eyed each other, I realized this was Albie's sign he had arrived in full. It was time for me to make another leap of faith as well, and he's been sleeping with us ever since.

As the bonds tightened between us — as Albie became an indispensable and joyous part of our lives, as we learned to trust him off leash in the woods along the Charles River and in the Berkshires of western Massachusetts where we spend a lot of time — I started following Greg Mahle on Facebook. There were so many heartwarming stories, a welcome respite from the onslaught of dreadful news that bombards us every day. One post particularly struck me: "As the miles melt away, so do a lifetime of bad memories," Greg wrote. "Lives of neglect, abuse, disease, kill shelters, starvation, and unspeakable cruelties. They are throwaways. They were unwanted, unloved, and about to die. But now they are getting a second chance. The promise of love, a family to call their own, and a warm bed to sleep in are ahead of us. Some of them have eyes filled with excitement, others have eyes filled with hope, and some are even filled with dreams. Gotcha Day [the day when dogs and families are united] and Forever Families are just over our horizon. It's a new beginning. Their time to be unloved and unwanted nevermore."

After reading that, I felt I wanted to know more about Greg Mahle. *These,* I thought, *are the musings of a man who has found a deep contentment that eludes most people in their lifetimes.* He seemed born to the job he was doing. We should all do work so meaningful.

But I also wanted to know more about Albie. He'd brought so much joy in the short time he'd been with us, and I wanted to know how he'd gone from being a random stray found by the side of a Louisiana roadway to a deeply loved member of our family. I knew there were some questions I might never be able to answer: Who had he lived with, and why did they let him go? Or, did he run away and leave some poor family to wonder about his fate? How long had he been alone? How had he survived?

But I also thought there were questions I could answer that would help me understand not only Albie's plight, but also that of countless other loving dogs without a place to call home. Where do all the dogs Greg drives north come from? Why are there so many southern dogs in need of homes, more than any other part of the country? Who walks the streets and the halls of the shelters and saves their lives? Who

21

are the people who extend their hands, and their hearts, to help Albie and thousands of others like him make the journey from central Louisiana or Texas or Mississippi to homes more than twelve hundred miles away? And why do so many people care so much that they will strain their marriages, their personal relationships, and their finances to help save dogs?

Those are the questions that drove me to find out more about Greg and the rescue movement — and, eventually, to write this book. I wanted not only to shed light on the plight of these dogs, but also to celebrate the unsung heroes of the rescue world and the families that give rescue dogs a second chance. And there was one man I knew who could help answer the questions I had: Greg Mahle.

So over the course of a year, I would join Greg for all or part of several rescue road trips, logging roughly seven thousand miles with him, cleaning kennels, walking and comforting dogs, and sleeping, with mixed success, on the trailer floor at night. But even if I hadn't wanted to do all this, Greg would have insisted because he knew it was the only way I could truly understand his life, his work, and what it takes to save a dog. Before he would trust me with his story, he needed to test my mettle and make sure I could do it justice.

I also spent time in four communities where many of the dogs Greg transports come from, getting to know some of the rescuers, the fosters, the veterinarians, and the volunteers who make each of Greg's rescue road trips possible. And, sadly, I walked through neighborhoods like Houston's neglected and impoverished Fifth Ward, where thousands of emaciated, flea-infested, mangy strays loiter, suffer, and often die in rubbish-filled ditches, boarded-up homes, and under the wheels of speeding cars. I also went to the shelters where dogs like Albie wait, usually in vain, for someone to fall in love with and adopt them; shelters where as many as 80 to 90 percent — even if healthy and of fine temperament — will be put to death due to overcrowding and lack of resources.

"People think it's so glamorous," Greg once told me, "that I'm playing with puppies all day." But a week on the road and you realize how grueling, stressful, exhausting, relentless, dirty, smelly, and demanding the work is; you have to get used to having dog poop smeared on your shirt and the smell of sixty to eighty dogs permeating your clothes. Just driving more than four thousand miles in six days every other week, let alone taking care of scores of dogs along the way, would test even the most determined person. If you wanted to be a trucker, hauling bottled water or auto parts would be infinitely easier. And he's doing it for considerably less than minimum wage to boot.

Despite the endless miles, the stress, the physical and messy work, and the sleeping in a trailer far from home for half of every month, Greg will be the first to tell you he has the best job in rescue. Every other week, he gets to deliver a group of lucky dogs into the arms of waiting families and see first-hand the happily-ever-after scenes that unfold at each Gotcha Day.

In addition to Greg, there are countless others who make these scenes possible, many of whom you'll meet in the pages ahead. They are the ones who turn stories of despair into stories of hope and give these dogs a first or second chance at love. They may never witness a Gotcha Day themselves, but they keep Greg running. They walk the floors of high-kill shelters; look into the baleful eyes of dogs that have been neglected, abandoned, and abused; save as many as they can; and lie awake at night, haunted by those they couldn't. They spend tens, sometimes hundreds, of thousands of dollars out of their own pockets to get these dogs healthy and ready for adoption, sometimes nursing them back to health themselves. They sometimes burn through marriages or relationships, or work eighteen-hour days while raising a family for so long that they can't remember a single day off. Without them, there is no Greg Mahle arriving in the Deep South to pick up eighty of the luckiest dogs in the world and bring them to safety. Without them, there are no joyful scenes in New Jersey, New York, Connecticut, and other states where expectant families, signs at the ready, look for Greg's big white truck and wait for their first glimpse of the once-forgotten dog they are about to welcome into their lives.

And for the dogs, whose long journeys began well before they ever climbed aboard Greg's truck, it is because of these people that their lives are about to change forever when Greg swings the doors open, scoops them up in his powerful arms, and places each one in the bosom of their new, loving family. This is ultimately their story too.

1
DOG'S BEST FRIEND

One winter night in 2005, after the last of five family restaurants he ran had closed and he was back in Mount Perry, Ohio, living with his mother, Greg Mahle received a call from his sister Cathy, the founder of Labs4rescue.

A paid driver was transporting a handful of dogs from the South in a van and was nearing exhaustion. She was on the interstate nearby. Cathy was desperate and asked if Greg could help rescue the rescuer and her dogs. A dog lover since he was a kid, he readily agreed and ended up driving all of them to Connecticut that night and into the following morning.

"It was awful," Greg tells me when I come to visit him in Zanesville, Ohio, where he and his wife Adella now live, to join him on one of his road trips. "There was just one woman with a bunch of dogs in this minivan and it smelled terrible." The trend of trans-

27

porting southern rescue dogs up north on a large scale was just beginning, a phenomenon that would accelerate as the Internet expanded Americans' understanding of the canine overpopulation problem in the South and facilitated match-making between dogs and families. "People were just winging it back then," he adds. "They were transporting dogs in open horse trailers, in overcrowded cars, you name it."

Greg had two revelations on that trip. First, the need for rescue dog transport was far greater than the supply, and second, he could professionalize and systematize what was largely an ad hoc, hit-or-miss system for moving dogs north. He started making occasional rescue trips with a van to help his sister and a few dogs, and he quickly became hooked. Soon, he was hiring drivers and running vans, a box truck, and a small truck with a trailer. He was on the road three weeks a month, but he soon tired of managing drivers and realized he wasn't comfortable leaving dogs in the care of others; he wanted to be hands-on and improve the conditions under which the dogs were moved.

"When I started, I was just a guy with a van giving dogs a ride," he says. "Transport has become much more professionalized since then."

But it also gave him an unexpected opportunity. "Before Adella and I became a couple, I was just going to live with my mother and cut hay," Greg recalls. "But now that we were together, I needed something to do and I knew I'd rather be a greeter at Walmart than go back in the restaurant business."

"The first couple of years, there were weeks he would borrow money for gas from me," says Adella. "It was okay with me because it wasn't much and I knew it made him happy. As time progressed and he was carrying more dogs, he eventually got to the point when he was able to pay for gas on his own. He always slept in the vehicle because there wasn't enough money to spend on a hotel room on the road. Back in the days when he had the vans, I felt sorry for him. Now that he has a trailer with a bunk, I don't feel nearly as bad. But he still complains sometimes about how cold it is on nights when he doesn't have dogs in the trailer because he won't run the heater, to save money.

"We still get by on a shoestring budget, a prayer, and a little help from God," she adds. Until 2014, Adella worked at the local Head Start agency, which helped with the household bills, but she left to pursue her master's degree in early education. "I still take odd jobs, teach a dance class, and do a little consulting with Head Start, and that's been enough to get us by. But every month, I say a prayer that we will be able to make it to the next month."

I first met Greg in September of 2013, about eight months before my visit to Zanesville, when I was covering Greg and his work for *Parade* magazine. I knew I wanted to share his story and hopefully encourage others to "think rescue" if they were looking for a dog. When *Parade* gave me the assignment, I traveled to Allentown, Pennsylvania, where I had arranged to meet with Greg and drive with him the next day to Putnam, Connecticut, the last stop of every Gotcha Day.

A genial man named Keith Remaly met me at the Comfort Inn just outside Allentown. Keith organizes the Allentown Angels, one of three groups of resolute volunteers who meet Greg and the dogs along the route every other week, without fail, to give each dog a long walk, food, water, and a whole lot of love. They help clean the trailer and the kennels and bolster the spirits of a road-weary Greg and his backup driver, Tommy, an imposing man at six foot five with a four-hundred-pounds-plus physique.[4]

Greg and Tommy, an air force veteran who always refers to Greg as either "Sir" or "Boss," drive through the night on Thursdays, into Friday, stopping occasionally to check on the dogs, walk them, give them water and snacks, and clean the kennels. On other nights, when they do stop for the

4. "Tommy" is a pseudonym for the actual person, who requested his real name not be used.

31

night, Greg sleeps in a tiny loft, on an old mattress in the trailer; Tommy, on a bunk in the cab.

Greg and I had been corresponding for weeks by email to arrange my trip, so I was a bit surprised when, meeting for the first time, he gave me a quick handshake and immediately handed me a black Lab puppy named Genesis and a leash. "Take her for a walk on the grass over there," he said, pointing to a field nearby. It wasn't a request; it was an order.

As I would soon discover though, Greg isn't gruff or unfriendly — quite the contrary. But the first thing you learn about Greg is: the dogs always come first. *Always.* Plus, there'd be plenty of time to get acquainted later. After all, we'd be riding almost three hundred miles together the next day.

That night, after the Angels had left and the dogs were all back in their kennels in the trailer, I approached a little back Lab puppy named Audi. I had chosen to follow Audi's journey for my *Parade* story because her short life was something of a miracle. She was one of eleven puppies (including Genesis) that were delivered to Blakely, who was found very pregnant and living by a Dumpster in New Iberia, Louisiana, and taken to a high-kill shelter. Like Albie, Blakely's first stroke of luck was being a stray, not a dog surrendered by its owner. Many owner surrenders, even if they are healthy, are euthanized at overcrowded shelters almost immediately because shelter personnel know no one is going to come looking for them. Strays can buy a few days on the assumption that if they are lost, someone is searching for them.

How any particular lost or abandoned dog defies the odds to ultimately find a forever home truly is a story of luck at every turn. On the surface, it seems simple: person finds dog, dog gets on truck, dog gets off truck into the arms of new family. But the story is always far more complicated. Very few people, even those with rescue dogs, know, or can even imagine, what it takes to do this work and the effort expended by countless people to get their dog to them safe and sound.

In Blakely's case, a Labs4rescue volunteer in Connecticut saw a cross-posted message online about a pregnant Lab in the shelter in New Iberia. She phoned two local volunteers who picked Blakely up from the shelter in their Ford Explorer. En route to the vet's office, she started delivering her puppies. Because they were born in a car,

Labs4rescue volunteers named each puppy after a car model: there was Chevy, Genesis, and nine more, including Audi, whose forever family, the Dooleys of Hamden, Connecticut, has since renamed her Brooke.

Audi and three of her siblings were along for this particular ride; Greg would later bring Blakely and the rest of the pups to their forever homes too. Since Audi and the Dooleys were the focus of my *Parade* story, I wanted to get to know her a bit, and I had promised the Dooleys I'd watch out for her and give her some extra attention, which she craved. When I put my finger through her kennel door, she couldn't stop licking and chewing it excitedly. I removed her from the kennel and she was a bundle of energy, squirming in my arms, licking my face, and nibbling on my ears. She didn't want to be let go so, with Greg's permission, I decided to let her sleep with me in the truck.

On the phone a week before I joined Greg in Allentown, I had offered to stay in the motel. I was trying to respect his privacy (I knew he slept in the trailer), but Greg was having none of it. I would sleep in the trailer. When it was time for us all to go to bed, Greg gave me his tiny loft, the part of trailer that hangs over the back of the tractor. It's about seven feet long, a few feet wide, and all of about three feet high. I took Audi and her kennel up there, played with her a bit, and put her in the kennel for the night, keeping her right next to my head. Greg was already asleep on the trailer floor — he goes out like a light — a worn blanket wrapped around his husky frame.

It was surprisingly quiet in the trailer. It took the dogs twenty minutes or so to settle in for the night, but once they did, it remained quiet, except for the hum of the air-conditioning and the occasional dreamer chasing a squirrel in his sleep. The lights remain on through the night. Audi, however, wanted so badly to be out of her kennel; she whimpered and whined for a good hour before we both drifted off for a very short night's rest.

Greg was up before first light to get ready for the big day ahead. I, on the other hand, stumbled out groggily and walked into the motel whose parking lot Greg uses as though I was a paying guest and washed up in the lobby restroom.[5] There are no amenities on the road when you're traveling with

5. The Angels meet Greg at the Comfort Inn, but he spends the night in another motel parking lot a short distance away.

Greg. His focus is solely on getting the dogs to their forever homes as quickly and safely as possible. So if you need to shower daily, this isn't the job for you.

We changed the paper in the kennels, washed off a few poopy dogs, and gave them all water and a small snack. They don't eat a lot on the journey for two reasons. First, they're under some stress and the motion of the truck can make a full dog queasy. Second, whatever they eat comes out the other end, and when you have eighty dogs in a confined space . . . Well, you get the idea.

As soon as the sun cracked the horizon, we were ready to hit the road. For dozens of families, this was the day they'd been waiting for: Gotcha Day. And it's the day when a week of drudgery, messy and stressful work, and the monotony of the road pay dividends for Greg in the joyful scenes that unfold at every stop.

Zanesville has been dying for as long as Greg can remember, ever since his days growing up on the rural outskirts of town. It's a story that has played out in countless towns in the heartland: once-prosperous communities buoyed by manufacturing slowly suffocating under the weight of globalization. Vacant lots, abandoned factories, and boarded-up storefronts now dot Zanesville like some kind of pox. Owens Corning, the fiberglass manufacturer, still has a small plant here, but today, Zanesville, which sits on the banks of the Muskingum River, is more notable for its commercial strip of fast-food restaurants and auto parts stores than its manufacturing base.

Greg and Adella and Adella's twelve-year-old son, Connor, live in a house in a historic section of town. The streets, paved with bricks in 1890s, are lined with stately homes. The Mahles share theirs with four dogs, all rescues: Harry, a golden retriever pulled from the Muskingum County Shelter, and three southern dogs: Murphy, an Irish setter from New Orleans; Treasure, a Carolina dog mix found in Tennessee; and Beans, purportedly a Lab-Rhodesian mix from central Louisiana, though no one knows for sure what's in Beans's DNA.[6]

6. The majority of rescue dogs are mixed breeds to some degree. Unless you have a DNA test done, determining breed(s) is typically an educated guess. Often the predominant breed is obvious, but since lineage is unknown, veterinary certificates for rescue dogs will often indicate

From the exuberance and tenacity with which he relentlessly plays fetch, he could be part Ty Cobb.

The Mahles bought their home four years ago, a large, nineteenth-century Italianate house onto which a Tudor front was grafted more than a century ago. From the backyard — fenced in to keep the dogs from running off — you can see the Muskingum River and downtown Zanesville. Except for a few modern touches, such as a couple of flat screen TVs and an Apple computer on Greg's desk, it's a home evocative of another era: fifteen-foot ceilings, stucco moldings, claw-footed bath tubs, dark woodwork, stained-glass windows, a multi-colored slate roof, cast-iron radiators, tasseled lampshades, and multiple sitting rooms surely called "parlors" a century ago. In this old house, the TVs and computers appear to be flotsam from a still-to-be-imagined future.

"LabX" or "beagleX" and so forth, the "X" indicating a mix to some degree or other. Unlike carefully bred dogs that often have nearly identical DNA, in rescue circles there's pride that every dog is truly unique. The motto of Mutts4rescue, a Rhode Island–based rescue organization that matches southern dogs with northern families, is "Love Knows No Pedigree."

If this sounds like a grand home for a man scratching out a living transporting rescue dogs, walk down Convers Street and you can find larger homes like this in move-in condition for about $150,000 and some in need of work for under $30,000.

Greg is an inveterate collector of "junk nicely arranged," as he calls it, and he continues to buy out of barns and thrift stores to furnish the house, proud that he can spend a few dollars and some time — when he can grab it — refinishing and have a functional and attractive piece of furniture. He proudly tells me he found the bed and two dressers in the bedroom where I'm staying in an old barn where they were covered in hay. The price? A grand total of ninety dollars.

"I cart home all kinds of junk," Greg says, "but they're treasures to me — like rescue dogs that are trash to some people, but treasures to me. I've always been this way."

When you're driving a truck long distances with eighty dogs, you have to be resourceful, and Greg is resourceful at home too. "I once hauled an old iron bed partly buried in a hog feedlot out with a tractor. I cleaned it up, used it for a while, and then sold it and used the money to buy a brand-new bed," he says, proud of the accomplishment.

There are various works in progress around the house, victims of Greg's life lived half on the road: a downstairs bathroom is far from completion and an ambitious, partly completed backyard patio awaits his attention.

The home, indeed the entire neighborhood, evokes Bedford Falls, George Bailey's hometown in Frank Capra's 1946 film classic *It's a Wonderful Life.* As I would learn during the course of the more than seven thousand miles we would ride together, "it's a wonderful life" is precisely how Greg feels about his own life, whether it's his two weeks on the road out of every month, or his two weeks at home with Adella, Connor, and the dogs.

Adella Mahle was only eighteen when she first met Greg some seventeen years ago. She was hired as a waitress at one of the five Brighton Ice Cream restaurants Greg operated with his mother in and around Zanesville. Greg is almost twenty years Adella's senior.

"My Dad owned a bar," Greg tells me as we drive around Zanesville one afternoon, two days before we're scheduled to leave Ohio for the Gulf Coast to pick up dogs. Greg, Adella, and I are in Adella's Subaru because Greg still drives a dilapidated white panel van he used in his early days in rescue dog transport. It has only two seats, a lot of miscellaneous junk rattling around in back, front tires of questionable integrity, a windshield riddled with cracks, a nonfunctioning air conditioner, a broken odometer, useless and tattered windshield wipers, and various holes in the dash where controls of one sort or another used to be. Greg *loves* this vehicle and sees no reason to replace it.

"Dad sold the bar and bought a building with plans to open a package store," Greg continues. "He didn't realize the building was too close to a nearby school to get a liquor license. The building had been abandoned and wasn't being used as a school, but the school district still owned it and he couldn't get the license."

So Raymond Mahle needed another plan and opened a small ice cream shop with a soda fountain in his would-be liquor store. Greg was in his early teens.

"He started offering a sandwich or two, and then another and another, and the next thing you know, you have a kitchen and you're in the restaurant business," says Greg. The first restaurant was located at the edge of the Brighton historic district in Zanesville on Brighton Boulevard, from which it took its name. The restaurant was a success, a testament to his parents' prodigious work ethic — a work ethic he inherited.

"I remember coming into the restaurant back in the early days," Greg recalls, "and there was my dad in the kitchen, sitting on a bucket, with a potato in one hand and a knife in the other, and he was sound asleep."

Shortly after the fifth restaurant opened, Raymond Mahle died. He was only in his midfifties. Greg, now in his early fifties, dropped out of Ohio University after two years and found himself in the restaurant business with his mother, Mary. Never much of a student, Greg figured he was going to end up working in the family restaurants anyway, so he cut his college education short.

Greg is very fond of his mother and they have a good relationship; he credits her with teaching him everything he knows about work and life.

"My mother and I worked together day in and day out for many years," he says. "I was lucky. We had disagreements, like what should be on the menu; she'd never take anything off even as we added new items. She was always sure there'd be one customer who might still want a particular sandwich, so we couldn't take it off!

"The restaurants taught me how to go to work each day," Greg tells me. "There was never a sick day and you worked long, long hours, sometimes fourteen or fifteen hours a day. It was hard labor day after day after day. I worked for years without a single day off. It prepared me for Rescue Road Trips, where I work twenty-hour days on the road. There are no sick days. And I learned to do it without bitching about it. I unload my complaints on Adella, and only on Adella," he says as she nods her head in agreement. But he describes dropping out of college as a poor decision. "When you're young, you think you have all the answers," he says.

For the better part of two decades, Greg and Mary ran the restaurants, working a grinding schedule, but Zanesville's decline continued, the national economy faltered, and tastes changed. The Mahles, by Greg's admission, failed to change with the times.

"Ten years ago, I hated the restaurant business. I hated *everything*," Greg tells me. "In the earlier days, when business was better, I was younger and stronger."

The restaurants started closing one by one, and Greg moved into an apartment he created in the sole surviving location. He and Adella had gone out together over the years, but it was nothing Greg considered a formal date. When the last of the restaurants closed, Greg moved back into the home where Raymond and Mary had lived since Greg was eleven, in Mount Perry, a little hamlet west of Zanesville.

"I had just enough to pay my bills," Greg tells me. "What more do you need? You can be close to broke and still be happy. I was dating lots of girls and hadn't seen Adella in about a year. Then I got a letter from her and I asked her out on a date."

Greg and Adella agree that she had been pursuing him ever since they'd met when she first came to work in one of the restaurants. Other than a little to pay the bills, he had no money, just a large jar of change, mostly pennies.

"So, to take Adella out on a date, I had to wrap the pennies and get dollars," he tells me. It was enough to take her to a Smith & Wollensky steakhouse at a mall near Columbus, and then to German Village, the old German section of Columbus where, incongruously, they drank tequila. To this day, Greg has several large containers spread around his home office filled with loose change.

Greg and Adella were together for about thirteen years before she finally persuaded him, in 2012, to get married. They had moved in together two years earlier.

"If I hadn't been very persistent, we wouldn't be where we are today," says Adella, who is petite, pretty, and sports shoulder-length hair dyed a brilliant red. Greg agrees. On the day they married, in July 2012, Greg returned from a week on the road at about three in the afternoon. The wedding was at six.

It's a relationship of genuine tenderness and mutual respect. Greg was well into his life transporting rescue dogs before they married, and though the bimonthly separations are hard, both are deeply committed to each other and the work. Adella helps Greg with countless Rescue Road Trips tasks and always sends Greg and Tommy off with a couple dozen turkey, ham, and cheese sandwiches to sustain them for the first few days on the road.

"I had been resisting Adella for years," says Greg, who'd been married once before. That marriage lasted about five years. There were no children. "I wasn't sure about the idea of marrying again and settling down in a family life."

Several years before they became a couple, Adella had Connor. When they married a few years later, he took his new responsibility as a stepdad very seriously.

"It meant buying a house, and now I'm going to be a stepdad and I'm going to have to step up to the plate for both of them," he tells me, his voice cracking slightly. "I needed to be good enough for both of them. I had known Adella wanted to marry me for at least ten years before we got married. Deciding to get married made me the happiest man in the world. I'm so happy being with this family and with what Adella and Connor give me. Sometimes we make each other madder than hell, but this is the greatest part of my life. It makes it much harder to leave every other Monday. I get a bit out of sorts on Sundays, but I also love my life on the road with dogs. Adella and Friday nights in the trailer with the dogs [the night before Greg unites the dogs with their forever families] are the two best things in my life. I love the life I have created."

"I hate it when he leaves," Adella says. "I've always hated it. But Rescue Road Trips is our life. Except for the very beginning, it's all we've known since we've been together."

Greg has no children of his own, but when he talks about Connor and his hopes for Connor's future, you'd be hard-pressed to tell Connor isn't his own son.

"I want Connor to go to college and get out of Zanesville," Greg told me as we drove from Columbus, where he'd met me at the airport a few days before we set off on a rescue road trip. "I don't have a college degree. I want him to work with his head, not his back."

When I met Connor a couple of days later — he had been spending the weekend with his dad — that wasn't hard to imagine. He's preternaturally bright and articulate and offered a stiff challenge when we settled down to a game of chess.

"I want him to have choices," Greg added, "and he won't have them in Zanesville." Adella wants Connor to grow up in Zanesville, where the cost of living is, fortunately, very low. Zanesville, says Greg, is "okay for now." Maybe that should be the town motto, we joke. Put up signs on the roads leading into town saying, "Zanesville: It's Okay for Now."

But once Connor's off to college, Greg fantasizes about where he might like to live. His thoughts are, quite literally, all over the map. He likes the idea of living in Manhattan, of being able to walk everywhere and not having a car. And he yearns for the anonymity of living in a big city, not surprising, perhaps, when you've spent your whole life in a small town where everyone knows you.

"Being with a thousand people on a street and being invisible, that appeals to me," he says. "I'd consider Alaska. I've never been to France, but I fantasize about living there." But Greg also intends to stay on the road, rescuing dogs as long as he is physically able, so those dreams will remain just that for the foreseeable future.

Greg is the second child of Raymond and Mary Mahle. He has two younger brothers who still live in Mount Perry: Scott, who works in a local factory but is training to be a minister, and Todd, a detective with the Muskingum County Sheriff's Office. His older sister, Cathy, the founder of Labs4rescue, works in pharmaceutical publishing and lives in Connecticut. Labs4rescue is one of the rescue groups that rely heavily on Greg to transport southern dogs to their new homes in the Northeast.

Before Raymond and Mary moved the family to Mount Perry, they lived in a single-story ranch home in the nearby village of Fultonham. Greg would walk a short distance to a bridge that crosses Jonathan Creek and fish for chubs using wadded up balls of white bread. Many days he would venture further, on foot or bicycle, to Lake Isabella, a man-made lake created in 1939 out of an old limestone quarry. The smoke stack of the now-defunct plant that used the limestone to make cement is visible from parts of the lake.

We stop by the Mahle family home in Mount Perry before driving down to the lake. The setting is bucolic. Rolling hills dressed in spring green form a small glen where the modest two-story clapboard house sits on a little knoll. The field across the street, which is part of the eighty-eight-acre property, is used to grow grass for hay. There is a large, worn-down barn, a remnant of an old dairy farm that predated the Mahles' occupancy, and a smaller barn beside it with an old tractor inside. A large brick cistern, used by the Mahles until they drilled their own well, sits on the hillside. There's not another house in sight.

Mary isn't home, but her dog, Pork Chop, is tethered outside and greets Greg and Adella with enthusiasm as we get out. We walk through the ground floor of the house; the kitchen wallpaper's design suggests it's been there since the 1930s or 1940s. Little else has changed since Greg wandered these rooms as an eleven-year-old.

We leave the house and drive a couple of miles down to Lake Isabella. For years, Greg spent almost every summer day here. There's a small beach, created by the county with imported sand. There's a recreation hall, a very basic free mini-golf course made from two-by-fours, a raft, a diving board, and a snack bar that serves up burgers, hot dogs, fries, and shakes. Greg's mother, Mary, operates the snack bar. As we munch on hot dogs on a perfect late spring day, Greg talks about growing up in a tiny town in southeast Ohio.

"There was only one kid my age anywhere near the house in Mount Perry," he says. "Her name was Vesta. One day I watched as a mule tried to run out of its stall in their barn, and she just knocked it out with one punch. I chose not to play with her after that."

Greg attended nearby Maysville High School and graduated in 1981, in a class of about eighty students. "I was a B and C student," he says. "I had the ability but not the ambition." He wasn't into cars and he was neither a popular kid nor an outcast. He had one particularly close friend in high school, also named Greg, and they remain friends today. "I didn't really fit in," he says with no trace of remorse. "I've always been my own best friend." Beer and girls — "lots of girls" — became his primary preoccupations during his high school years. But he also loved dogs.

When he was in third grade, a stray dog followed him home from school. As was common in that time and place, Poochie, as the mutt became known, lived outside the Mahles' home.

"My dad wasn't happy," says Greg. "Poochie had seizures that caused her to foam at the mouth. She stayed around for a couple of years and then just disappeared." Poochie would become just the first of many strays to live in and around the Mahle household; by Greg's reckoning, he and his brothers brought home at least a dozen, some smuggled in under towels, over the years.

"We found them on the street and fed them, and they lived on our porch," Greg tells me. "This was forty years ago and that's how it was done."

In addition to the strays, the Mahles had many "official" dogs. Raymond Mahle liked to hunt birds and had many hunting dogs that also lived outside, Brittany spaniels, English setters, and Irish setters.

"My affinity for Irish Setters," he says, referring to his own, Murphy, "came from my dad." But taking in the strays really made an impact. "It's how I learned that taking care of dogs felt good," he says.

Pork Chop was also a stray Greg pulled from the Cambridge, Ohio, pound. At first, Mary wouldn't even let the dog in her car. Years later, when Greg, with some trepidation, told her he was moving in with Adella, she was matter-of-fact: "You can live together, but the dog is staying."

When Greg talks about the feeling he gets from bringing rescue dogs to safety, he thinks back to Poochie, his first stray. "That's the feeling I'm always trying to recapture," he says.

On the Saturday before our departure for the Deep South, there's a major chore to be done, and though it's usually done earlier in the week, Greg has postponed it so I can see what goes into preparing for each rescue road trip. I knew from my brief ride with him the previous fall that there are no human passengers on his truck, only workers; if you're there, you're there to help with whatever needs to be done. And before I flew out to Ohio, I emailed to assure him I understood it was "all hands on deck" while I was riding along.

During the week, I would learn the work

never ends and the demands of transporting eighty dogs in a tractor-trailer is dirty,
sometimes dangerous, exhausting, and
unrelenting. Today would be my first taste
of just how much backbreaking work goes
into each trip well before a single dog gets
on board.

We hop into Greg's white panel truck, the
one Adella calls his "creepy stalker, rapist
van" because other than Greg, she thinks
that's the only kind of person who would
own such a wreck. Our first stop is Sam's
Club, the discount buyers' club, where Greg
picks up five one-gallon spray bottles of
Clorox Clean-Up. From there we head for
Mattingly's parking lot, a local trucking
concern where Greg rents a parking space
for his rig for a hundred dollars a month.
It's gated and secure. We park the van and
Greg fires up the tractor. It has to run for a
few minutes before it can be driven, to allow pressure to build up in the brake lines.
While the truck idles, Greg checks the three
gas-powered generators strapped to the
platform behind the cab, the generators that
provide power to run the four air-
conditioning units and heater in the trailer.
Each costs $2,000 and is secured only by
the straps, so parking the rig in a fenced
and locked lot is a small insurance policy

against theft. Mattingly's also has a full-time mechanic who can fix Greg's truck on the premises, a major convenience.

Once the truck has warmed up, we drive about a quarter mile to a field adjacent to a service station. Greg pays them a hundred dollars a month too, to park in the field and to connect hoses to their water supply. This is where the trailer and all eighty kennels will be thoroughly disinfected and cleaned before we depart. This requires removing every kennel from the trailer — some, for smaller dogs, easily carried, others more cumbersome — and placing it in the field. The trailer is forty-eight feet long and "Rescue Road Trips: Saving Lives Four Paws at a Time" is emblazoned on both sides together with a large photograph of a young woman holding out her hand and looking tenderly at a black Lab.

Fortunately, it's a beautiful day — warm but not hot, with tolerable humidity. Still, the job will take four of us — Greg, Adella, me, and Adella's mother, Debbie, who is one of Greg's two salaried employees (Tommy is the other) — five and half hours to complete. That's a lot of time in the sun, and as the work proceeds, I ponder the fact that this job has to be done in brutal heat and humidity in summer and on bitter winter days because Greg runs every other week without fail. In the winter, Greg tells me, a thin layer of ice will form in the buckets Debbie uses to wash out the kennels. He's seen her reach down and crack the ice with her hands before she continues working with the frigid water.

We quickly fall into our respective jobs. Greg, using a portable, hand-powered pump, sprays Clorox Clean-Up to disinfect each kennel, and I rinse each with a hose. Inside the trailer, Debbie and Adella sweep the trailer clean. A lot of detritus builds up in the trailer during trips — soiled newspapers in trash bags, flat tires, and miscellaneous donations of dog food, toys, and other paraphernalia. All that is placed in the field, to be sorted out or discarded.

Once the trailer is empty and swept, Greg sprays down the interior with the disinfectant, and then the entire inside of the trailer is hosed down from top to bottom. Once that's done, Greg and I continue with the kennels, placing the clean ones at the trailer's back door, where Debbie and Adella begin the process of putting them back in position and securing them, using bungee cords, to rails along the trailer walls.

By the time we're done, I have my first taste of the physical work involved in Rescue

Road Trips. Then, I get a surprise. Greg tells me the job that just took four of us more than five hours to complete was often done solo by his mother-in-law, but she's since hired a nephew to help her. I ask Greg if there aren't laws in Ohio against mother-in-law abuse. I can't imagine one woman in her sixties, with arthritis no less, doing this job alone.

Greg says Debbie, who is also Greg's go-to on-call person 24–7 when he's on the road, is the hardest-working person he's ever seen. Typically, she spreads the cleaning of the trailer out over several days; she is plodding and methodical and keeps at it a few hours at a time until she finishes. When he's on the road, it's Debbie who will call all the adopters if he's running behind schedule, deal with any changes in the reservations, help him find the nearest roadside assistance in case of a breakdown, and do any other task Greg needs help with. She also manages all the office paperwork.

"To people adopting dogs, Debbie is invisible," says Greg, "but what she does is essential." Indeed, this will become a theme Greg returns to often during our trip: the countless people who play a vital role in securing the life and the freedom of each and every rescue dog, people who, unlike

56

Greg, won't get any credit, whose names will never be known, and whose work will never be seen. Part of my goal on this trip, and others to come, is to make them visible, to show just how many people and how much work play a role in saving the lives of the dogs Greg drives north.

On Sunday, the day before we are to leave Ohio for the long drive to the Gulf Coast, Greg makes waffles and link sausages for breakfast. When you're a guest in the home of a man who once ran five family restaurants, you can count on hearty food. Greg doesn't believe in opening a package and saving some for later. If he opens a package of sausages, he's going to cook them all. I wonder if I can afford the calories given that I suspect our diet for the next week isn't going to win any awards from Weight Watchers.

The TV in the kitchen is tuned to CNN, but it's mere background noise. Greg and Adella aren't watching and neither am I — nor are any of the dogs. Greg has his laptop at the table and is preoccupied checking reservations for the upcoming trip. Rescue groups make reservations online for each dog being transported, much as you might book an airline ticket. Invariably there are last minute changes: dogs come down with an illness that delays their travel, someone has a last-minute addition, an adopter backs out, etc. The final passenger list will be in flux even as we are on the road.

It's quiet in the house, save for the TV and the sound of an occasional passing train on the tracks down the hill from the Mahles' house. As if Zanesville didn't already seem like a town from America's industrial past, Greg tells me those are coal trains coming from the mines in southeast Ohio, near the West Virginia border, headed for a coal-fired electric plant to the north. Zanesville is neither a mining town nor a farming town. Though there are farms about, it straddles a space between Ohio's coalfields to the south and east and its corn fields to the west.

Treasure lies on the bench at the kitchen table, a long, wooden table salvaged from an old donut shop. It still has an industrial-grade cast-iron can opener bolted to one end. Harry is curled at Greg's feet. Beans and Murphy are occupying themselves in the backyard.

Beans is a relentless ball hound. One evening, after dinner on the patio, I tossed him the ball and he went at it in a frenzy, retrieved it, and, with a quick upward flick of his muzzle, tossed the slobber-covered ball directly into my lap. Then he backed up with rapid stutter steps, growing more and more agitated with every passing second, waiting for me to toss the ball again. By the time I picked the ball up out of my increasingly damp lap, he was quivering with anticipation so intense I thought he might explode. We repeated the process dozens of times, and had I been willing, it seemed as though he could have gone on all night.

When Greg takes a break from his laptop, I ask him what the Sundays before he leaves are like for him.

"I don't dread or look forward to the Mondays when I leave," he says. "I'm stressed. Have I taken care of all the details, so that nothing blows up on the road? The week between trips is actually more stressful for me than the week on the road. When I'm home, I feel like I have to do everything people ask of me. On the road I can say no."

Even on the off weeks, Greg spends anywhere between sixty to eighty hours on rescue road trips. And I'm partly to blame for a recent increase in the pressures on him. After the *Parade* piece was published in March 2014, Greg started getting a barrage of phone calls and emails. It seemed everyone and his brother had something they wanted from him: ideas for a reality TV show, business plans, get-rich schemes, even marriage proposals. "From women *and* men," Greg wrote to me that spring. "My email has been interesting to say the least."

Then the *Parade* piece spawned a spot on *The Today Show,* and months later Greg was still busy trying to be polite by responding to everyone — even those he thought were just eating up his time. But he knows the publicity helps spread the word about rescue, and Greg is nothing if not the Elmer Gantry of dog rescue, preaching his gospel to anyone and everyone who wanders by his truck while he's on road, greeting each with a hearty, "Hi, I'm Greg," even if he's in the middle of changing a tire or working with Tommy to get eighty dogs out one or two at a time for walks. When we were cleaning the trailer, half a dozen curious passersby wandered over, and each received a hearty Greg Mahle greeting and some words about rescue dogs. Then, he'd patiently answered their questions until their curiosity was satisfied.

"Now that Adella isn't working and is home, she can do more to support me," Greg tells me, "so it's made Mondays easier. But I don't like leaving Adella, Connor, and the dogs. And I know, come next Saturday night, I am going to hate the lifeless feeling of the trailer after all the dogs have been dropped off."

After breakfast, Greg and Adella and I attend Sunday services at their church. Greg was raised a Methodist, Adella a Catholic. They belong to the Grace Methodist Church in downtown Zanesville, a five-minute drive from their house.

For many years, Greg stopped attending church, partly because of the seven-day workweeks he was putting in at the restaurants. But when he and Adella married, and he became a stepfather, faith once again became a priority.

"I wanted Connor to have the childhood I had, and church was a part of that. Going together as a family brought my family closer together, and I wanted that for him. The family ritual and the memories it creates are big parts of going to church for me.

"So I felt the need to return to the church," Greg tells me. "I didn't want to go back to the church I went to as a kid, and one day I was driving by Grace and saw a sign out front that they were having an early morning service the next day. The early morning services are held in the basement, because they aren't as well attended as the

61

later service, and Adella and Connor and I started to go.

"I felt God was calling me home to the church," he adds. "I needed to add religion and faith to my family. Having and practicing faith gives me comfort. And having a church to call home does too. It makes me feel good right now, today, and it makes me want to strive to be more of what God wants me to be. Practicing faith helps me to be a better person. Just like baseball practice makes you better at the game, practicing faith helps me to be better at life."

Greg's dog-saving mission isn't a religious one, but it's informed by his Methodist faith with its tradition of helping the less fortunate.

"God wants good things for all people and animals," he says. "Helping a dog is God's work, but I don't see my work in religious terms. If I see a person who has fallen, I should help him stand up. If I see a dog that needs help standing up, I should help that dog stand up. Rescue Road Trips isn't a religious mission; it's just rooted in my religion — you help those in need."

I ask Greg: With so many children in need in this country and around the world, why dogs?

"That's a tough question," he admits.

"There are lots of people in need and lots of problems in the world. But you do what you can do, what you are capable of doing, and I can help dogs. And I'm helping the people who adopt them, but really it's the dogs I'm helping. I may not be changing the world, but for each dog I help save, I've changed the world for that dog.

"I try hard to be a better person," he says. "To have more faith, to do more of what God wants me to do. There's always room for improvement. With me, there's a *lot* of room for improvement."

On the eve of our departure, Adella makes spaghetti with meat sauce and the four of us — Greg, Adella, Connor, and I — eat at the kitchen table. *These are really good, hardworking people,* I think to myself, *who value each other, hard work, and the food on their table.* The life they've chosen, one that requires repeated separations and reunions, isn't an easy one, but there's no complaining. Tomorrow will bring another separation. But now, it's time for another helping of comfort food.

2
ON THE ROAD AGAIN

When I come downstairs the next morning, Greg is standing with his fists resting on the kitchen counter. He has Popeye-like forearms and a sturdy build; he looks like a guy who could lift an ox and carry it into the next field if he had to. Of average height, about five feet nine inches, he has a round, welcoming face with cherubic pinch-me cheeks, and a full head of tousled brown hair worn relatively short. He uses drugstore reading glasses Adella buys in bulk because he's always losing them. Today he's wearing his warmer weather road uniform: cargo shorts, sandals, a blue "Rescue Road Trips: Saving Lives 4 Paws at a Time" T-shirt, and a tattered, beige baseball cap, adorned with the same words as his T-shirt. At the counter, he appears to be deeply contemplating a cup of coffee.

"Usually I throw up the morning I have to leave," he tells me. "It's the stress. I'm

usually yelling to Adella to do this and that. But today I feel unusually calm. Maybe it's because you're here."

I don't take this as a compliment; maybe I've just been enough of a distraction to keep him from dwelling on what I surmise is the real source of this anxiety: leaving Adella and home yet again. Though they've made this separation hundreds of times, it doesn't get easier.

Greg's goal is to get to the truck about 2:30 p.m., leaving several hours to attend to last-minute preparations. But this being the Mahle household, it begins with another important ritual first: a substantial breakfast of muffins, cereal, and a pound of pepper-crusted bacon. Murphy makes ten quick circles before settling into a spot on the floor; Harry makes less of a production of it, but he too has chosen a spot. Beans, as usual, is in a ball frenzy, repeatedly dropping his slobbery ball into my lap. I've been here three days and I'm almost out of clean shorts thanks to Beans. I don't know where Treasure is hiding.

After breakfast, Greg runs out to the drugstore to pick up some medications, and I watch Adella pack his bag for the week. I think I've packed frugally, but Adella puts me to shame. She packs three T-shirts, one pair of jeans, one pair of shorts, one towel, three pairs of reading glasses, and a couple pairs each of underwear and socks. There's not even a change of shoes.

It's a warm, sunny day with a nearly cloudless sky. At midday, Adella makes a pasta salad for lunch; I rarely eat so well at home. Greg typically doesn't eat lunch on departure days; he's too nervous and his stomach can't handle it. But today he feels calm enough to enjoy his wife's cooking.

After we cleaned the trailer on Saturday, we put about a dozen trash bags and a couple of broken-beyond-repair kennels into Greg's white van. Today, while Greg is attending to email, Adella and I haul this trash to the curb for pick up. The last chore is the making of the sandwiches, the two-dozen (with a few extra because I am coming along this time) ham, turkey, and cheese on pita rounds sealed individually and put in a cooler to sustain Greg and Tommy for the first couple of days on the road.

I throw my bag into the van, which we'll drive to Mattingly's, and say my good-byes to Connor, who is home because it's a school holiday. I'm convinced he still isn't happy about losing to me in chess, but to my surprise, he asks when I can come visit again.

The drive to Mattingly's where the truck is parked takes less than five minutes, and we're there around two. Adella follows us in her Subaru. As Greg checks the generators, the running lights and the tires, Adella climbs up into the small bunk at the front of the trailer and puts clean sheets and blankets on Greg's mattress. The bunk is no place for a claustrophobe; you can't sit up in the space and there isn't a single window in the entire trailer. Back in the fall, Greg insisted I sleep there while he slept on the floor. There'll be no such luck this time; after my trip to Allentown, I'm now a veteran of sorts and will be down on the floor in a sleeping bag between the kennels at night.

While we wait for Tommy to arrive, Greg checks to make sure each kennel is tightly secured to the walls of the trailer. He asks me to put one piece of yellow duct tape and one piece of purple on each kennel; the yellow will be used to write the name of the dog in that kennel and the purple to number each kennel. Greg hasn't fired up the generators yet, so it's warm inside. By three fifteen, Tommy has arrived and we're still preparing for departure. Already I need to shower which, Greg informs me, I can do when we reach Virginia on Friday, four days from now. Greg and Adella embrace and say goodbye yet again. Finally, just before three thirty, with Tommy at the wheel, we ease through the gates of Mattingly's and jump onto Interstate 70 West, heading toward Columbus.

The goal is to reach Bowling Green, Kentucky, this first night, but we'll drive farther if traffic is light and we're making good time. A mile driven today is one less mile to drive tomorrow, and it's a long way to Alexandria, Louisiana, over a thousand miles from Zanesville. Not even a hundred yards out and Greg gets the first of the countless phone calls he receives on the road. It's about picking up a dog slightly off our route. Greg usually tries to be accommodating and will, if he has time, make small detours to help a dog escape the South, but this trip, for the first time in months, he's fully booked.

For half an hour, Greg and Tommy compare notes on the respective relics that serve as their main means of transportation when they're not in the truck, but Greg's van seems assured of the top spot when it comes to derelict vehicles still capable of movement. Tommy extols the virtues of Walmart pork chops fried up on the stove, and then we pull off the highway in Newark, Ohio, just twenty-six miles from Zanesville, to fill up with diesel.

When he gets back to the cab, Greg shows me the receipt. He's taken on 146 gallons of fuel. The cost is $590 and we'll travel about a thousand miles before we need to refuel. That's about a dollar in diesel for every two miles, not to mention gasoline for the generators. I assume the generators are needed to keep the trailer cool in summer and warm in winter, but only the first part is completely true. Greg tells me when the outside temperature is four below zero, the body heat and breath of seventy dogs will keep the trailer at a comfortable seventy degrees. The challenge is keeping the trailer cool when they're driving through the scorching heat of a southern summer; then, all four air-conditioning units have to be run full blast around the clock.

When we were driving from the airport in Columbus to Zanesville a few days earlier, and Greg mentioned how broke he was when he first took Adella on a formal date, he also told me, "I could care less about money. Do I have enough food for today? If so, then I'm OK. I just want to do things that make me feel good. I get happiness from picking up the dogs and from my family. That's all I want. I don't give a shit about money."

Of course, a lot of people will profess not to care about money, even when they do. Since he's shown me the fuel receipt, it seems as good a time as any to broach a subject I've been unsure how to open. Just how much money can a guy make doing this job?

As I soon discover, the math is pretty daunting. As we roll on toward Cincinnati, I begin to get a sense of how expensive it is to run the rig. Greg bought the tractor used a few years ago for $20,000, sight unseen, from a man in Vermont, and he and Tommy flew to New England and drove it back. It had about 450,000 miles on it, but these trucks, he explains, can go a million miles or more before the engine needs to be rebuilt. The odometer now reads close to 800,000 miles. But he's driving over 8,000 miles a month and the oil needs to be changed after every two to three trips. That's over $200 a pop right there. In summer, when sizzling hot roads take their toll on the trailer tires (the *tractor* tires are nearly invincible), Greg averages about four tire changes per trip; an average of one tire change (which he can do in seven minutes) in cooler weather. That's $800 in tires on every summer trip or $1,600 a month. Just after Christmas 2013, the clutch failed near Hattiesburg, Mississippi. With a trailer full of dogs, Greg was forced to idle for two days. As word spread via social media (Greg posted the news on Facebook), volunteers started to materialize to help Greg take care of the dogs. But the clutch was still a $7,000 repair. And there's insurance of course, Tommy's salary, Debbie's salary, taxes, fees paid to every state the rig passes through, and dog food, though that is sometimes donated. To break even, Greg needs to transport about fifty-five dogs on a run, and there are times when he has a light load and makes the entire trip without a dollar in profit to show for it.

How exactly does it all work? Rescue organizations make reservations online, though there are always last-minute additions and subtractions managed by phone. Debbie prints out a passenger manifest that, in a few days, will look like a line-up card created by a particularly indecisive baseball manager. Greg charges a flat fee of $185 regardless of where the dog is being picked up or dropped off, and whether it's a five-pound Chihuahua or a hundred-pound Lab. The transport fee is part of the fee adopters pay for their dog to a rescue group such as Labs4rescue, Mutts4rescue, or Houston Shaggy Dog Rescue, the three groups that account for the lion's share of Greg's business. It's slightly higher than some other dog transporters charge, but as Greg says, "When you use Rescue Road Trips, you get me. I am with your dog 24–7."

When he's on the road, Greg is effectively working a twenty-four-hour day for six straight days. Even when he's catching a few hours' sleep in the trailer with the dogs, he's on duty. That's a 144-hour workweek, and he makes the trip every other week. When he's home, he works an average of sixty to eighty hours a week. All told, that's more than four hundred hours a month. When you do the math, he's making less —

significantly less — than minimum wage, even when he has a full load.

"I could make more money flipping burgers at McDonald's," he acknowledges. If he didn't love the work, if he weren't on a *mission,* it would make absolutely no sense — no financial sense anyway. "My salary is whatever is left over after expenses," Greg tells me. "In the first three months of 2014, because of repairs and light loads, I didn't make a dollar. But the restaurant business taught me to live with the ups and downs."

One of those downs came a few years ago, when his previous tractor, purchased new for $67,000, turned out to be a lemon and brought him to the edge of bankruptcy. One day, as Adella was heading to the grocery store, Greg gave her the bad news he'd been concealing for too long. The checking account was empty and all three credit cards were maxed out. They were dead broke. Adella was so stunned, she had to hold on to the kitchen counter for support. Then, Kathy Wetmore, the founder of Houston Shaggy Dog Rescue, stepped in, paid $7,000 from her own pocket for that clutch repair he charged in Mississippi to keep Greg on the road, and Greg and Adella recovered.

Greg may not care about money for himself, but to keep the truck rolling and to keep saving dogs, he has to think about the bottom line because he doesn't have deep pockets to finance the operation himself. Though Rescue Road Trips is a limited liability corporation, not a charity, he gratefully accepts donations. I have seen a few adopters hand him a gratuity, but he doesn't do any active fund-raising.

One of the reasons the Mondays he starts a trip are so stressful is that the size of the load is still in flux and will remain in flux until the last dog boards later in the week. The stakes are high. Will he have enough dogs on board to cover costs? If there's a late cancellation, he refunds his fee, which strikes me as overly generous since he can't always fill a slot at the last minute. On some trips, the cancellation rate can be 10 percent, which can mean losing more than $1,000 in business if he's unable to fill those vacancies. "It's just the way I was brought up," Greg says. "If I don't do the job, I don't want the money."

He also has future costs to think about. Though he's only had the current trailer for two years — in addition to the $20,000 he paid for it, the trailer needed about $7,000 in retrofits to make it usable for transporting dogs — it's near the end of its useful life. It's a former race-car trailer, not one made for repeated long-haul trucking. Greg wants to replace it with something called a "Kentucky double-drop" trailer. A used Kentucky double runs around $18,000, but by the time it's retrofitted for transporting dogs, the cost could easily double. Greg's unofficial, pro bono engineer-in-chief is John Bradley of Connecticut. John's wife, Sue, is a regular volunteer at Greg's Rocky Hill, Connecticut, drop-off point. It was John who helped Greg find the tractor in Vermont, and it's John who advises Greg on how to squeeze more miles from the current trailer until he can afford another.

When Greg claims not to give a whit about money, he means what he says and says what he means. In fact, that's true about Greg in general. Ask him a question and you'll get a thoughtful, direct answer. With Greg, the bullshit quotient is exactly zero.

By late afternoon we're making our way past miles and miles of cornfields on the outskirts of Cincinnati. The land is flat and the billboards are filled with ominous, religious messages. "If You Died Today, Where Would You Spend Eternity?" and "Hell Is Real" are two that catch my eye.

We've only been on the road two hours

and Greg is already missing Adella "like crazy," and second-guessing his interactions with Connor during the week he was home. "I wasn't patient enough with him," he says to me. "I didn't spend enough time with him. I have to do better with him."

He's also a little miffed at Keri Toth, for whom he's transported dogs for years from Louisiana. He adores Keri, but she works so hard and cares so much, she's often scrambling at the last minute to figure out how many dogs she'll be sending up and that wreaks havoc on Greg's ability to manage the reservations.

But he's over some of the anxiety that often causes him to throw up before he leaves. "It's the stress of everything. I hate leaving my family. I worry: Will Tommy show up? Will the trailer be okay? Are the reservations in order? It's not one thing; it's everything. It's a good week when I don't throw up." Greg will remain tense to a greater or lesser degree, however, until Friday night, when he arrives in Allentown. Getting the dogs safely to their new homes weighs just as heavily on him as his love for his family.

"By Friday nights, the dogs and I have become a unit, a pack," he tells me. "We're safely out of the South, and if something happens to me or the trailer, we're close enough, so they'll still get to their forever homes one way or another. I know they're all going to make it and I can exhale."

Soon, Riverfront Stadium, home of the Cincinnati Reds, comes into view on the left. Tommy is still behind the wheel, and the ride is punctuated by phone calls in and out. As we roll across the Kentucky line at six thirty in the evening, Greg calls Adella using his hands-free headset and asks her to pass along some pick-up information to an adopter. There are calls about cancellations, new reservations, and pleas to make room for just one more dog. When you run on the thin margins Greg does, every reservation and cancellation matters, so you take the calls.

As I listen and observe all this, one thing becomes clear: the rig isn't just a way to transport dogs; every other week, it becomes Greg's office, his home, and his mission. When there are dogs in the trailer, the truck is attended by Greg or Tommy every minute; to ensure the dogs are always supervised and safe, they won't even go into a truck stop restroom at the same time.

In between phone calls, Greg gives me a little tutorial on the details of dog transport.

Every dog needs a U.S. Department of Agriculture (USDA) health certificate signed by a licensed veterinarian. Greg, too, has to have a USDA license to transport animals and a U.S. Department of Transportation interstate commerce license. Though the USDA permits dogs as young as eight weeks to be transported if accompanied by the mother, Greg has stricter rules: dogs must be twelve weeks old and have three rounds of shots for parvovirus (a highly contagious canine virus) and distemper (also a virus). They must be heartworm negative (though the tests aren't always 100 percent accurate), negative for bordetella (kennel cough), and have a negative fecal exam.

He also talks, as he often does, about the people in canine rescue whose faces you never see and whose names you'll never know. His sister, Cathy, for example, the founder of Labs4rescue, the organization that united us with Albie, saves countless dogs she never sees or touches. With her husband, Harvey, they spend countless hours reviewing adoption applications, organizing field volunteers who pull dogs from shelters for adoption through Labs4rescue, organizing home visits, and navigating the bureaucracies in the various states where they are placing dogs.

"We are all cogs in a wheel in rescue," Greg explains. "Everyone has a role to play." Though he's had his share of publicity lately because he's the lucky guy who gets to play Santa on Gotcha Day, he's aware he's just one small part in a much larger movement and is quick to give credit to others. "You can't be in this for praise or glory. I'm in it because I want to see the dogs and pat their heads. Cathy and Harvey don't get to do that, but their jobs are so important. The shelter manager who gives a dog just a few more days, hoping someone will adopt him, is important. The veterinarians and vet techs who provide free care are important. My mother-in-law who cleans the trailer, she's important. John Bradley, who does the engineering, he's important. The angels that show up in Birmingham, Allentown, and Rocky Hill, they're all important. No one's job is any more important than anyone else's. It takes a hundred people playing their roles to save a dog. The adopter is the last link in the chain. That's why I thank each adopter for saving a life."

The especially hard work, though, is done by the people who pull dogs from high-kill shelters, patrol rural Dumpsters and city streets where dogs are often abandoned or where they congregate looking for scraps, or intervene when there's hoarding or a dog-fighting situation and find sixty or seventy dogs living in terrible conditions in a squalid home. When Greg first got into canine rescue transport, he was sometimes picking dogs up directly at city and county shelters. Now, because he's transporting so many dogs, there are central pick-up points: in Alexandria, for example, a Pizza Hut parking lot next to veterinary clinic that cares for many of the dogs going on Greg's transport is the pick-up point. In Lafayette, it's the shelter operated by Lafayette Animal Aid, a humane organization. In Hammond, Louisiana, it's another veterinary clinic.[7]

As he describes some of the horrors he's seen, I pay close attention. I'm trying to prepare myself for the weeks ahead, when I'm going to spend time with the people doing the really heart-wrenching work, often deciding which dogs to save and which will be left behind.

"At some shelters," he tells me, "county prisoners do the labor and use high-power

7. Since my travels with Greg, his route and some of the stops have changed, as they do from time to time, to respond to increasing or decreasing demand.

hoses to clean the cages." Many have large drains, Greg explains. "Sometimes, I don't know if it's intentional or not, they'll wash puppies right down the drain. I've seen some facilities where they'll back a truck up to a sealed-in space where they have the dogs and run the exhaust until they're all asphyxiated.

"I saw hope in the eyes of the older dogs who were about to die," Greg says. "The puppies are less expressive. Sometimes they throw dogs into the gas chambers on top of the dead ones, and still they look at you with hope.[8] I don't know if they know it's a gas chamber, but even when the door closes, they're still looking at you with hope. And I've even seen dogs piled into a drum and burned with diesel fuel in Georgia and then they just stir it a bit with a pole.

"There are puppies being killed by the thousands," he adds. "Some people look at them and see a disease-carrying animal to be gotten rid of. Black dogs have it the worst, because they're less popular." For reasons that are unclear, black dogs are the hardest to place in adoptive homes, yet they are just as sweet and loving as any others.

8. More and more states are banning the use of gas chambers to euthanize dogs.

It's a bias without justification, but a harsh reality nonetheless.

Greg is still haunted by the faces of some of the dogs he saw going to their deaths years ago.

"I still see the little Chihuahua who was looking up at me from behind the bars," he says. "The dogs know something awful is going to happen, and they're howling and barking and crying, and this little dog looked up silently at me, right at my eyes. I told him 'I can't help you,' and I think he knew I was his last hope. He just laid his head on the ground. He understood me. I will never in my life forget that Chihuahua."

At that moment, Greg faced a dilemma all rescuers who pull dogs from shelters face: deciding who will live and who will die. It's an excruciating experience but a reality in the grim math of rescue. The number of dogs is simply overwhelming, and you can't take them all, even though you want to. I think of the sign we passed a few miles back: "Hell Is Real." Now I believe it.

Greg doesn't pick up directly at shelters now. He's become more organized and more efficient, as has the entire rescue movement. In the old days, Greg was "scooping up dogs" everywhere and saw more of the shelter world; now, by the time the dogs are picked up, they've been moved to safety by dedicated people doing really hard work. Still, my sense is that these horrific images of the past are a big part of what binds him to his mission.

"My goal," he says, "is simply to get dogs north [to their adoptive homes] as soon as possible."

Why so many southern dogs? There are several reasons. First and foremost — especially in the rural South but to some degree in more urban areas too — there is no strong culture of spaying and neutering dogs. Some people avoid it because they feel it deprives dogs, especially males, of one of life's pleasures. But this means a large number of their dogs' offspring may be destined for lives of deprivation. They may be left to fend for themselves, die by a road, or end up in a shelter to be euthanized because the owners don't have the resources or any interest in taking care of them. That's a high price to pay for a dog's sexual pleasure. Many dogs, even those with owners, also live outside, where they can wander and mate freely, creating more offspring that people don't want.

Another reason for the high number of shelter dogs from the South is that in many parts of the South, dogs aren't seen as companion animals, as they mostly are in the North, but rather as livestock or property. If they are supposed to fulfill a function — as a hunting dog, for example, or a guard dog — but prove ill-suited for the task, they are simply abandoned or worse. And there's a lot of backyard breeding, people hoping to make a few dollars peddling puppies. If they can't sell the puppies, they abandon them. It's a deeply rooted and complex cultural and social problem we will explore further.

To be sure, there are lost, abandoned, and abused dogs that need homes in every state, but the problem is far more acute in southern states. There's no influx of dogs from Connecticut and Massachusetts, for example, to Texas, Alabama, and Louisiana, and no transports such as Greg's filled with dogs heading south from the North. The reason is simple. The oversupply is in the South and the demand is up north. Transporting rescue dogs to the South would be like delivering coal to Newcastle.

As we roll along, it's hard for me to imagine the monotony of driving the same 4,200-mile route every other week. How many times has Greg noted the sign that says

"Louisville 100 miles" and passed the next two hours waiting for Louisville to come into view only to count down the 175 miles from Louisville to Nashville? How many times has he pulled into the same Flying J truck stop, had a cup of coffee from the same place, and passed the same hillsides and cornfields?

The land gets hillier in Kentucky, and for a while we drive in silence, the radio tuned to a country music station. For some reason I'd forgotten in the months since I first rode with Greg from Allentown to Putnam, to write the *Parade* piece, how rough the ride is in the cab of a big rig. Driving five hundred miles in a truck like this is far more tiring and punishing than five hundred miles in a car. Even for a passenger, the relentless jostling is exhausting, like being in a plane in continuous turbulence. It's why my notes look like they were written by an especially jittery five-year-old.

The traffic has been light all afternoon and early evening, and the weather clear, so we're making good time. Greg announces we'll make it past Bowling Green and push on past Nashville. Better to stop on the far-side of it, so we don't have to deal with rush hour traffic going into the city in the morning. It's 7:00 p.m. when we eat the first of

Adella's sandwiches.

Greg's in the mood to vent a little about the pressures he's under, especially now that word has been spreading about him and his organization. People have started to see him as some sort of savior for every lost canine soul on the planet.

"I get calls all the time like, 'I've got a dog and I have to give him away and no one will take him and you're his last hope. If you don't take him, I'll have to bring him to the shelter,' " Greg says. "People try to guilt me into taking their dogs all the time. People email me pictures to try and get me to take their dogs. I can't take all these dogs! I wish I could, but I don't have the right place to put them all."

He's inundated with requests, and his natural instinct is to want to help everyone. He feels beleaguered, but only a man frustrated that he can't respond favorably to every request would feel that way. If he didn't care, the requests rolling in would keep on rolling, right off his back.

By 8:00 p.m. we're on the ring road around Louisville and merge onto Interstate 65 South, headed for Nashville. Half an hour later, Greg calls Connor. Before he left,

Greg hid some whoopie pies in a drawer for Connor's dessert. Now he tells him to go look in the drawer to discover the treat. It's just a small way of staying connected when he can't be home.

We're traveling along a stretch of highway dubbed the Kentucky Bourbon Trail and pass signs directing people to the distilleries of some of the most famous names in whiskey: Jim Beam and Maker's Mark among them. Dusk has settled over the increasingly hilly terrain as we pass the exits for Fort Knox and Abraham Lincoln's birthplace in Hodgenville.

As nightfall nears, Tommy pulls the truck over and switches places with Greg. Tommy's driven us 310 miles; Greg will take us past Nashville.

As we approach the western half of the state, the clock drops back one hour. We're now in the central time zone. Greg drives us about 150 miles until we stop for the night at an enormous truck stop in Fairview, Tennessee. We've come 457 miles from Zanesville. There appear to be more than a hundred tractor-trailers parked in rows in the expansive parking lot, their engines idling. Parking is on a first-come, first-served basis, but there's no fee to spend the night; truck stops make money selling fuel, food, and truck repair services.

Within five minutes of slipping the rig into its parking space, Greg is in his bunk in the trailer, fast asleep. Tommy is in the bunk in the cab, and I am spreading out my sleeping bag on the unforgiving floor between the two rows of empty kennels. Except for the sound of the air conditioner, it's eerily quiet. Without windows, it's like being in a submarine, seemingly cut off from the outside world. The generators send gentle vibrations through the trailer as I lie awake thinking about the dogs that will soon be joining us.

I've gotten pictures and know a little about some of the dogs who, in the next two days, will begin a journey that will change their lives — and the lives of their adopting families — forever. There's Tennessee, a three-year-old yellow Lab mix who lived with a homeless man under a highway overpass for two years before his owner surrendered him to a shelter, hoping he'd find a way to a better life. (Ages are estimates based on overall appearance and indicators such as tooth wear and tartar buildup.) There's Trudy, a deaf and blind Catahoula mix, and her close companion, Popcorn, a Hound mix, both pulled from a high-kill shelter in Alexandria, and Bijou, a two-year-old beagle mix, a stray pulled from the Saint Martin Parish Animal Services shelter, also in Louisiana. And there's Willis, described to me by his foster mom and Kathy Wetmore, his rescuer in Houston, as the world's happiest little dog. The day after tomorrow, we'll start picking up these and about seventy-five others, and the trailer will spring to life. But right now, it has the feel of a theater set waiting to be populated by the actors.

All day I've been focused on learning as much as I can from Greg about operating Rescue Road Trips and getting a sense of the rhythms of his bifurcated life. Now I'm starting to imagine the trailer filling up with dogs, each with a story to tell, most of which will remain a mystery. Every stray dog has a past; maybe it even included a family. But if no one claims her, no one will ever know. A dog left tied to a fence or dropped in a Dumpster had a life, but one no one will ever know the details. If dogs could talk, oh the stories they'd tell. It takes a while but around one in morning, a couple of hours after Greg has fallen quickly into a deep sleep, I finally drift off myself.

At six the next morning, Tuesday, I wake up

and crack the side door to the trailer. It's light out, so I grab my shaving kit and wander through canyons of tractor-trailers to the truck stop's main building which houses a large convenience store, a TV room, laundry facilities, a Denny's restaurant, and thankfully, restrooms.

As I walk in past guys with beer bellies testing the limits of their T-shirts; scrawny guys with greasy NASCAR caps, sunglasses, and tattoos; and a surprising number of women truckers, I feel like a foreigner in my own country. I'm sure it's obvious to everyone that I've never been to a truck stop in my life, especially because my Teva sneakers, shorts, and Ithaca College T-shirt, all betray the fact that I'm in unfamiliar territory. From the looks of it, I may also be the only one who has ever carried a shaving kit to a truck stop restroom.

Greg and Tommy are being so generous letting me tag along that I'm determined not to cause them a minute's delay if I can help it. So I quickly take my medications and brush my teeth. On my way out to the truck, I pass Greg on the way in. I'm relieved. The last thing I want to see is him behind the wheel, Tommy in the passenger seat, both looking at their watches saying, "Where the hell is that guy?"

By six thirty, Greg is back behind the wheel, and we're driving west on Interstate 40 toward Memphis.

When Greg is driving, Tommy is usually glued to his droid, playing video games on the tiny screen. Sometimes, Greg tells him to stop, get in the bunk, and rest up so he can drive safely when Greg tires. When Tommy drives and Greg isn't taking calls or posting to Facebook, he spends much of the time gazing out the window, lost in his thoughts until I interrupt his peace with yet another question, which he generally tolerates well. In fact, he seems happy for some relief from the boredom; it's not as if he's admiring scenery he's never seen before. I ask him about the dangers of driving so many miles.

"I've had a lot of close calls on the road," he says. "Been cut off many times. One time, coming west on 84 in Connecticut, there was a crash in the eastbound lane and I suddenly saw a tire hurtling through the air, coming right at me, and it just missed."

Obviously he can't control what other drivers do, but he can control how safely he operates. He can sleep or catnap while Tommy drives and makes sure Tommy gets the rest he needs. Though he is dubious

91

about its effectiveness at preventing sleepiness, he drinks lots of coffee and at night sleeps soundly. If both men are too tired, they pull off the road and sleep; they know their limits.

But of all the hazards beyond their control, weather is the most worrisome. "I've seen it rain sideways in Texas and snow in Louisiana," he tells me. "Interstate 10 was shut down. People were so excited, they were making snowmen on the median strip."

It can be especially bad in the winter in the South because road crews are ill prepared for snow and ice. Greg was stuck in northern Alabama for twelve hours once when the roads iced over. And a Virginia blizzard once stopped him for three full days on Interstate 81.

Greg didn't have the large trailer then, so he was driving a box truck with thirty-six dogs, all Labs. He thought he could get ahead of the storm, but near Staunton he was forced off the road and into a truck stop; it was too dangerous to go on.

"My first concern was safety and staying alive," he tells me about the harrowing conditions on the highway. "So at first I was relieved when we got into the truck stop. But I had no idea we'd be stuck for three days." The storm was so bad, the highway was closed.

Greg always has about a week's worth of food on board, so that wasn't a concern, and the body heat and breath of the dogs kept the truck warm enough for him to sleep in a T-shirt. But the snow was hip deep and getting the dogs out to pee and poop was arduous. Eventually, they wore narrow trails through the snow, just wide enough to walk the dogs one at a time. But his only pair of boots got waterlogged and then froze solid when he left them near the door.

The other worry, of course, is the health and safety of the dogs. Greg has transported well over thirty thousand dogs from the South. Only once did a dog have to go to a vet. When he reached Allentown on a trip about six years ago, he noticed one of the dogs seemed lethargic. It could barely stand up and walked as if it were drunk. One of the Allentown Angels who worked as a veterinary technician took the dog to the vet, where it was diagnosed with diabetic shock.

Inevitably, dogs have died on transport too, but of the thirty thousand plus dogs he's transported over the years, only five didn't make it. Even dogs that meet all legal health requirements for transport, and Greg's higher standards, can have undiagnosed ailments that don't manifest until they're on transport. And Greg believes good screening by the rescue groups he works with and his own attention to the dogs' comfort and happiness contribute to the extremely low mortality rate.[9]

As we roll on toward Memphis, we pass signs advertising Loretta Lynn's Ranch and Kitchen and the Bucksnort Trout Ranch. By 10:00 a.m., we've passed Memphis and less than half an hour later, cross the Mississippi border on Interstate 55 South headed for Jackson. It's an overcast day, a blessing for Greg and Tommy, since it's much easier than driving with the sun beating through the large windshield.

Late in the morning, Greg gets an email from Kathy Wetmore of Houston Shaggy Dog Rescue, the woman who once saved Greg and Adella from bankruptcy by paying for a very expensive new clutch for his truck. Marvin, a three-year-old dachshund mix, has a slight cough and can't travel this

9. Assuming 30,000 dogs and five fatalities, that's a mortality rate of .00002 percent. To look at it the other way, it means Greg has safely delivered more than 99.98 percent of the dogs he has transported.

week. Kathy is, rightly so, an absolute stickler about such things. I know this means a single young woman in New York City, Anna Wright, is going to be deeply disappointed. A few days earlier, I'd spoken with Anna by phone. She made her decision to rescue a dog after seeing the piece about Greg on *The Today Show.*

"It just tugged at my heartstrings," she told me. When she saw a picture of Marvin online, she thought his "little face was the sweetest thing I ever saw." Marvin was a day or two away from being euthanized when Kathy pulled him from the shelter operated by Houston's Bureau of Animal Regulation and Care, or BARC. Marvin's owner surrendered him, perhaps because he had contracted a severe case of heartworm, which, though thoroughly preventable, can be difficult and costly to treat. Kathy assumed that responsibility and the expense before she put Marvin up for adoption.

"Marvin will make my apartment my home," Anna told me, "not just the place I go to at night. He'll be my family. He'll be my partner in crime."

Late cancellations are par for the course, and Greg takes the news in stride. But once again, it's the uncertainty surrounding how many dogs Keri wants on this transport that's causing Greg to worry. In addition to about a half-dozen Labs4rescue dogs, Keri calls Greg and says she now needs an additional thirty slots for dogs bound for a big adoption event to be held the coming Sunday in Warwick, Rhode Island. Keri adopts out a lot of dogs through Mutts4rescue, which is based in the state.

"You just never know exactly how many dogs you're going to have until you get there," Greg says to me, "there" meaning the pick-up points in the South. "We always make it work somehow, but I'm very stressed out about it. Some weeks I'm stressed because we have a light load, which means we may not break even. Other weeks, we have a heavy load, like this week, and I'm stressed about how we're going to manage it. It's very hard to hit the sweet spot in between."

In a pinch, there are a few extra kennels holding supplies that can be pressed into service, and some larger kennels can accommodate two dogs, but at the moment, it appears there are going to be nearly ninety dogs on this trip, including the thirty Keri wants to send to Rhode Island. Greg knows Marvin won't be the only last-minute cancellation, but right now he's like a man possessed with a Rubik's Cube, trying to solve the puzzle of ninety dogs and about eighty kennels in his head, a puzzle made more complex because he hasn't seen the dogs and won't know how many of the passengers will be large breeds, such as Labs, small breeds such as dachshunds, or medium-size breeds such as griffons. There will also be a mix of older dogs and puppies. It's like three-dimensional chess.

"Ideally, I want one dog in one right-sized kennel, but some weeks you just have to improvise," he says. Siblings, and there are usually several, can typically share a larger crate without difficulty, but there are no hard-and-fast rules if some dogs need to share a kennel. They may even be switched around en route, to give those riding in pairs more room for part of the journey. "I will not just put a couple of dogs in a kennel," Greg tells me. "I will make sure each one is comfortable."

People picking up their dogs in the Northeast often expect to see a sparkling clean trailer, an equally fluffy and clean dog, and perhaps even a clean-shaven and freshly showered Greg Mahle. That's simply impossible with sixty to eighty dogs on the road for three to four days. And some think having dogs share a kennel is cruel. But every dog you can get on transport makes room in a foster home or a no-kill shelter for another dog that might otherwise die. However, Greg is not trying to squeeze on every dog he can, and he won't transport a dog if he doesn't think it can be made comfortable. There are just some weeks, and this in one of them, when the load is a bit heavy and he has people pleading with him to take one more. So if it means that some dogs have to bunk up for a couple days to ensure that others can live and hopefully make it to forever families too, Greg is willing to do it.

"You just have to live with uncertainty," he says, "and have faith on each run it will work out." Although it "somehow always works out in the end," it isn't helping Greg's high blood pressure at the moment. He tries to focus on Friday night, three days away, when his bonding with the dogs will be complete and he will have reached Allentown with Gotcha Day just hours away.

At midday, the overcast Mississippi sky of the morning gives way to clear skies and fluffy white clouds. Kathy Wetmore texts that Houston, where we are headed tomorrow after the first pickups in Alexandria, has been hit by severe weather that caused extensive flooding and some road closures.

That weather is now headed east into Louisiana, where we will be in just a few hours.

"It's rain, not a hurricane," says Greg, "so I assume the interstate [Interstate 10, which runs east-west across southern Louisiana and into Texas] hasn't been closed." But Greg knows severe weather can mean heavy wind gusts: if they are coming straight on, it's not a big problem; if they are coming sideways, it's manageable; but winds gusting at an angle to the rig "will have you hanging on to the wheel," he tells me.

By the time we reach the tiny town of Waterproof, Louisiana, the skies have grown eerily black and the rain is pounding down. Waterproof is getting drenched. The view out the windshield, the wipers flapping madly, looks like something out of *Storm Chasers*. Fortunately, the predicted winds and hail fail to materialize and the rain eventually relents, but it's a reminder that Greg is very much at the mercy of the elements, whether it's the heat and severe weather of the sultry South in summer, or the ice and snow of the Northeast in winter.

Right around 6:00 p.m., we reach the truck stop outside Alexandria where we'll spend the night. Greg has done all the driving today, 586 miles, and he's beat. He takes a call from Keri, who still can't give him a final count even though we start loading first thing in the morning. But, she assures him, most are puppies and can share kennels. Even without the final count, Greg knows every kennel will be full this run, only his second full load in the past five months.

Before bed, we shoot the breeze for a little while. He tells me if it weren't for Adella and Connor, he could happily live his life on the road full-time. And I discover he finds many of my questions, designed to help me understand and organize the opaque world of canine rescue, miss the point. It's a community so diffuse, so random, and so chaotic, and rescue work is done in so many different ways by so many different people and organizations, it's impossible to generalize about.

Shortly after nine thirty, Greg climbs into his bunk. Tommy's been asleep for two hours in the cab. For the second night, I lay my sleeping bag on the hard floor wedged into the twenty-eight-inch-wide aisle running down the middle of the trailer between the two rows of kennels stacked two and three high. When I turn my head to the side, my nose is about three inches from one of the kennels. It's not nearly as comfortable as it sounds.

By this time tomorrow night this cocoon, infused with the hum of the air-conditioners and the thrum of the generators, will be alive with dozens of barking, whining, and crying dogs. But, if the one night I spent on the road with Greg the previous fall was any indication, all will settle down soon enough, and we'll fall together into a peaceful sleep.

3
ALL ABOARD

We're up at six thirty the next morning and make the short drive from Alexandria to Pineville to pick up Keri Toth's dogs.[10] It's warm and humid; the skies are heavy and threatening. The exact number of dogs Keri will have on transport is still unknown and Greg is in high dudgeon. He loves Keri and admires her deep commitment to saving dogs, but she doesn't make his life easy.

The problem is that there are a fixed number of kennels and many dogs to be picked up down the road. Keri's indecision means Greg has no idea how many dogs she plans to board, how many he'll have all told, and how he's going to get them all on board and in circumstances that will be

10. Greg lists Alexandria as the pick-up point on his website and always refers to it, on Facebook and elsewhere, as Alexandria, but the actual location is in Pineville.

comfortable for them and for the other dogs he's picking up. Experience tells him he'll figure it out, but it's still stressful each time he has to go through this. He also knows from experience that Keri will be organizing the necessary paperwork at the last minute. He's concerned it's all going to add up to a delay that will cause him to run late all day and there will be people and dogs waiting in Baytown, Texas, our next stop.

Shortly after 7:00 a.m., we pull into a Pizza Hut parking lot across from the Haas Animal Hospital, the staging area for loading the truck. After two nights on the road with an empty trailer, I'm excited to start meeting the dogs and seeing how Greg manages the morning's chaos with Keri. The predictability of traveling with two human beings is about to be irrevocably altered by the exhilarating unpredictability of traveling with dozens of dogs. The ride south has given me a chance to ask Greg countless questions about his work, but now the action is about to begin.

Some of the dogs have been staying at the clinic for several days, some have been brought from foster homes, and others collected the day before from the public animal shelter in Alexandria, where they'd been given a reprieve pending adoption.

The first dog to board is Tippi, a tiny two-year-old shih tzu. Greta Jones, a local volunteer with the Humane Society of Central Louisiana (HSCL), of which Keri is president, brings her to the side door of the trailer.[11]

11. In truth, the HSCL *is* Keri Toth, Greta Jones, and a handful of volunteers; it has no offices, no staff, no phone number apart from Keri's, and no formal budgeting or fund-raising processes, just debts owed to local veterinarians who treat the animals Keri and her volunteers rescue. When I

104

Greta hands me her iPhone and asks me to take a picture of her and Tippi. Tippi has lived with Greta for a year, and Greta's eyes fill with tears as she hands the dog up to Greg. I'm sorry for her. Tippi, on the other hand, seems unfazed and doesn't resist or squirm. This parting is far harder on Greta than on the dog she fostered.

It's my first hint of the emotional investment people like Greta make in this work. Greta fosters several dogs at a time, and like many who foster, she clearly faces the pain of this separation repeatedly. But it's what they endure to save the lives of these dogs. The good news is that Greta knows Tippi is headed to a forever family in Rhode Island who will love her deeply. When Greg puts her in one of the small kennels at the front of the trailer, she scratches at the metal mesh door, the first sign that she's upset. Does she know she's saying good-bye to Greta? Can she sense her grief? Or does she

---

visited, Keri was in the process of merging HSCL into the CenLa (Central Louisiana) Alliance for Animals (CAFA), another scrappy rescue organization run by Sara Kelly, a highly energetic, determined, multi-tasking physician and mother of two young daughters. The two organizations merged in the late summer of 2014.

just want out of the kennel? I have no idea, but the scene is heartbreaking and inspiring at the same time.

Next to board are some Labs4rescue dogs bound for forever homes as well: Duchess, an eight-month-old black Lab, and then a puppy pair: Nikki and Natalie, four-month-old black Labs. Puppies are used to being in close quarters with their littermates. As anyone who has ever watched a litter of puppies knows, they sit on each other's heads, flop and fall all over one another, and sleep huddled close together. So doubling them up in the kennels won't bother them; it will likely provide some comfort and companionship during the long journey. Greg is feeling better about accommodating each dog in comfort because Keri has many sets of puppy siblings among the forty dogs she's going to board. But at every stop, Greg will check to make sure the dogs appear content together. If there are signs that dogs sharing a kennel need to be separated — repeated nipping, restlessness, or constant scratching at the kennel door, for example — he'll make changes.

With about half a dozen dogs boarded the skies open up and it begins to pour. With nearly three dozen more waiting to be loaded onto the truck, we're going to have a lot of wet dogs and wet people by the time we finish, but I'm struck by how calm the dogs are as they get on. The puppies are easily passed to Greg or Tommy and offer no resistance as they're put into their kennels. Those large enough to climb into the trailer do so matter-of-factly, some eagerly, as if they can't wait to get going. I didn't expect the dogs to be so malleable and cooperative; after all, they don't know us, and there's a lot of commotion to put them on edge.

But it all changes suddenly when a man referred to as Mr. Robin, a vet tech at the Haas Animal Hospital, leads Teddy, a seven-month-old shepherd mix, to the trailer.[12] Found a few months ago in a cow pasture with an emaciated mother and nine littermates, Teddy is wary of the trailer. You can see it in his posture as he slinks forward, ears flat, and in his fearful, furtive gaze. Just as Mr. Robin lifts Teddy up into the truck and Tommy reaches out to take him by the

12. Robin is his first name. In parts of the South, including central Louisiana, it is still common, as a sign of respect, to refer to people this way. I was introduced and referred to often as "Mr. Peter" while there.

collar, Teddy lashes out, snarling, biting, writhing, and involuntarily urinating and defecating everywhere. Greg yells to Tommy to release his grip. For about thirty seconds, it's pure pandemonium as everyone tries to subdue Teddy without hurting him or getting hurt as he strikes at anything that comes near him. Then, as quickly as it began, it's over. Teddy tumbles out of the truck and flops onto the pavement and lies so still Greg thinks for a moment he's dead. Greg watches as Mr. Robin, someone Teddy knows, crouches over him and strokes his head and back. He lies still with his stomach flat on the pavement. When it's clear Teddy isn't hurt, just scared, Mr. Robin gently leads him back to the clinic, where Keri decides he'll need more socialization and individual attention before he's ready to travel.

Then I notice Greg rubbing his hand. Teddy has nipped Greg, just a mark, no blood, an unusual but not unprecedented occupational hazard. Mr. Robin has been bitten too, but his wound is thankfully superficial also. The whole episode is so terribly sad. There doesn't seem to be anything vicious about Teddy; he was simply overcome by fear. Greg tells me scenes like this are extremely rare in his ten years of experience. But for me, seeing the boarding process for the very first time, it's stunning. Because events like this are so rare, Greg hadn't even thought to tell me it can occasionally get a bit dicey.

Tommy and Greg work quickly to remove Teddy's waste from the truck floor, so we can continue loading. We have several hundred miles to drive to pick up dogs this afternoon in Baytown, outside of Houston, and then back to Lafayette, Louisiana, so we'll be ready first thing tomorrow morning for pickups at Lafayette Animal Aid.

In addition to ten Labs4rescue dogs and six Mutts4rescue dogs, Keri now wants to board two-dozen dogs for the Rhode Island adoption event to be held this coming Sunday, but she's only made thirty reservations in all. Adding to Greg's frustration, dozens of the dogs haven't even been microchipped yet — injected with a tiny silicon chip readable by a scanner that can be used to identify the dog if it ever becomes lost — so Micheal Mitchell, a vet tech at Haas Animal Hospital, is injecting the dogs with their chips on the truck after they've been loaded.[13] This adds to the delay, much to

13. That's not a typo; he spells his first name Micheal.

Greg's chagrin.

And with Micheal in the aisle between the kennels, it makes it hard for Tommy to keep loading dogs that have been micro-chipped already. Ideally, all this should have been done in advance.

Greg isn't sure how he's going to manage if he lets Keri board ten more dogs than she has reservations for, but he keeps his cool and gently reminds Keri he wishes she were more organized. It's a discussion they've had before and seem destined to have again. Keri is always playing catch-up, and constantly on the move; if a dog needs to be rescued, paperwork is going to wait. Eventually, Greg relents, his frustration with Keri outweighed by his respect for her and his love for the dogs. He tells Keri she can board them all. As I would learn in the days and months ahead, improvisation is a constant in all aspects of canine rescue work, and as we make our pickups down the line, Greg will figure out how to accommodate every one.

Molly, a seven-year-old basenji mix is next. Keri tells me she was found with sixty-nine other dogs in a horrific hoarding situation Keri intervened in. Some of the dogs were bleeding, many had severe mange, a potentially lethal skin condition caused by parasitic mites that cause severe itching, and some were so vicious they eventually had to be euthanized. What some of these dogs have endured beggars belief. I have a strong urge to apologize to them on behalf of the human species and assure them better days lie ahead, at the end of the ride they are about to take.

Keri has been fostering Molly herself until finally, after a year and half, she found someone in Connecticut willing to foster and hopefully help Molly find a forever home. Why send Molly to another foster home rather than wait for a forever home? Just moving one animal from foster in Louisiana to another in Connecticut frees up a space at Keri's house for yet another dog that might otherwise be put down. So even though Molly's next home won't necessarily be her forever home, it ensures she'll be well cared for and another dog will be allowed to live.

When Keri explains this to me, it really hits me how crucial foster homes are to the rescue process. This is very much a one-dog-at-a-time, step-by-step process and fosters, whether in the South or up north, play a critical role in keeping the rescue train running. Fostering can also be a good way to make sure a dog is compatible in your household if you're thinking of adopting, but it also comes with the responsibility of taking an active role in finding a forever home if you aren't going to keep it. Many people who foster proudly become "foster failures": they fall in love and keep the dog.

Next on the truck are Popcorn, the hound mix, and Trudy, the young Catahoula. A distinctively Louisiana breed named after Catahoula Parish, Catahoulas are known for their loyalty and gentle, loving temperaments. They are a medium- to large-sized breed and the state's official dog. Trudy was born deaf and almost completely blind and is very attached to Popcorn, with whom she was fostered. Trudy's owner surrendered her to the Alexandria shelter; Popcorn was a stray who landed there too. Perhaps because of her impairments, Trudy is a bit ungainly and rambunctious. But because she's so attached to Popcorn, Greg decides the two will share one of the larger kennels for the trip north. Trudy and Popcorn are part of the group bound for the Rhode Island adoption event, a group that includes another dog Keri boards, T-Bone, a beautiful one-year-old black-and-white fox hound–pointer mix, one of six puppies dumped on a rural road with their parents in Natchitoches Parish in northwestern

Louisiana. A family nearby called animal control and agreed to take the parents. A neighbor agreed to care for the six puppies while they searched online for a humane society to help, and within a few days the puppies were all in Keri's custody.

Siblings Jupee, a black Lab mix puppy, and Pam, a chocolate Lab mix pup, are next, two of the group that has come to be known as the "tub puppies."[14] They too are bound for the Rhode Island event and look as healthy as puppies should, but their health belies their backstory, which is even more frightening than most.

On a cold morning in March, Micheal, the vet tech, came to work early with Mr. Robin and found a sealed, unventilated five-gallon Rubbermaid tub at the clinic door. There was no sound or movement coming from the tub, but when he peeled the cover off, he saw fourteen small puppies huddled together. From the condensation on the bottom of the lid, he knew they'd been there most of the night, surviving only on the oxygen inside. Eleven were Lab mix puppies about five weeks old, and three were

14. Because these are not purebred dogs, it is not uncommon for siblings to be of varying colors.

rat terrier mix puppies about four weeks old.

Normally Micheal comes to work at seven thirty, but he arrived early that morning to clean kennels and feed animals being boarded at the clinic. It proved fortuitous because the puppies' temperatures had dropped into the low nineties (normal is about one hundred); they were on the brink of freezing to death, shivering and lethargic. Once they got the puppies to the treatment area, Micheal and Mr. Robin warmed towels in the dryer, grabbed heating pads, and filled soda bottles with hot water and inserted them into socks, so the puppies could huddle against them. Slowly, the puppies' temperatures started to rise, and within the hour they started to whine and cry, a welcome sound. Micheal mixed a little milk with what he calls "A.D." — a diet high in nutrients used to feed critical-care animals. ("A.D.," he told me, means "almost dead" in rescue speak.) It is a food of last resort, and if animals refuse this or are unable to ingest it, they will almost certainly die. Micheal could only pray the puppies would eat it. To his relief, most of them took to the mixture, though some had to be syringe fed.

When Dr. Bari Haas, the clinic's founder,

arrived shortly thereafter, she examined each of the puppies. All had gastrointestinal parasites — hookworms and/or roundworms — and had to be dewormed (deworming is accomplished by means of an orally administered medication).[15] Given their young age, they likely contacted the parasites in utero from their mothers or through the mothers' milk. Dr. Haas later told me it's not uncommon at her clinic, and others in the area, to nurse back to health dogs and cats that were found leashed to a post, tossed over a fenced enclosure, or left at the doorstep in baskets or kennels. While this may sound indescribably inhumane — and it is — at least this shows some conscience on the part of the owner or whoever left them; countless others are simply abandoned in woods or by roadways or Dumpsters, or, perhaps more mercifully, shot.

When they were strong enough, Micheal took the three rat terrier puppies home to foster. "But I'm a bad foster," he told me. "A few days after I brought them home, I decided to keep them." All fourteen of the

15. Heartworms, unlike roundworms and hookworms, invade the heart and treatment is longer, more complex, more costly, and in many cases, riskier than the treatment for parasitic worms.

tub puppies survived. The commitment of people like Micheal can restore your faith in humanity; that he and Mr. Robin were able to save every single one of the tub puppies seemed nothing short of miraculous.

Finally, the S puppies board last: Sally, Sylvia, Sully, Seth, and Salyna, three-month-old Lab mix siblings from a litter of ten born in a rural area fifteen miles outside of Natchitoches. They were born to a silver lab mix mama who belongs to the Nash family. Salyna is the only yellow one (she also has a lot of white); one is silver, and the others are black. Salyna's face is as sweet as a baby harp seal's, and surprisingly, she has an entirely blue tongue. At first I think maybe she's oxygen deprived but am assured by Greg that some dogs just have solid blue tongues.[16] She's handed up to me, to pass to Tommy, who is now putting dogs in kennels about midway down the trailer. She seems especially nervous — she's trembling — so I pull her close and she lays her head

16. Contrary to popular belief, a blue tongue doesn't necessarily mean a dog has Chow Chow in its DNA, a breed known for its blue tongue, but it suggests the dog may have some Chow Chow in its lineage.

on my chest, one paw draped over my shoulder. For me, it's love at first sight. For Salyna, I'm sure, I'm just a warm shoulder to lie on. Like many of Keri's dogs on this trip, she's also bound for the adoption event in Rhode Island. We have our moment and I pass her to Tommy. Best not to get too attached.

Whenever there are groups of dogs in kennels, whether in the trailer or shelters or yards, the appearance of people invariably sets off a relentless cascade of almost unbearable, blood-pressure-raising barking and howling, unless, like Greg and Keri, you're accustomed to it. A few dogs will remain calm and quiet, but most will join the chorus. Now, as we finish loading the last of Keri's dogs, all the activity and commotion has sent the dogs into a barking frenzy. Even those that were seemingly calm getting into the truck have caught the fever.

Consider this: A normal conversation between two people is conducted at about sixty decibels. But like the Richter scale, which is used for measuring earthquakes, increases in decibels are exponential, so seventy decibels, where a typical dog's bark begins, registers one hundred times louder than sixty decibels. According to Alexandra

Horowitz, author of *Inside of a Dog: What Dogs See, Smell, and Know,* a single dog bark can spike at 130 decibels. Put eighty dogs in a trailer or shelter, and the racket can be excruciating. People who work in shelters or in rescue have to work amid this noise all the time, and if you're trying to communicate with a coworker, you can shout and still not be heard over the din. As the truck has been filling up, the din has been growing louder and louder.

By 9:30 a.m., we've loaded all forty of Keri's dogs. Typically, she doesn't have this many on Greg's transport — the average is between ten and twenty — but the Rhode Island adoption event has swelled the numbers. And that's not all: In addition to the two-dozen adoption event dogs we have on board, Keri and Greta will be driving another forty to Rhode Island themselves, mostly puppies and small dogs, in a van. They're hoping to return home in an empty van, each dog successfully adopted.

This will be a high-stakes event for Keri: like many rescue organizations, the Humane Society of Central Louisiana operates on a shoestring. Before she can complete a planned merger with the CenLa Alliance for Animals — "so we can be bigger and better," says Keri — she has to pay off over

$10,000 in debts owed to two veterinary clinics, including Dr. Haas's. She's hoping the adoption fees collected in Rhode Island can help close this gap.

It takes another hour to make sure the paperwork for all forty of Keri's dogs — interstate health certificates and other medical records — is in order. At 10:30, later than he hoped, Greg is ready to get moving again. The next stop, 225 miles west, will be Baytown, Texas, on the outskirts of Houston. For all the dogs we've boarded this morning, their final journey home has begun. There are many miles for them to travel still, but for so many others who will never find their Keri or their Greg, this is the road not taken. All I can think of those on board is, *Lucky dogs.*

4
SAVING DOGS

All of those lucky dogs now in the back of the truck had come from *somewhere* and I knew they had beaten long odds to be at the door of Greg's trailer on that warm, rainy morning in Alexandria. But I wanted to know where they had come from and *how* they wound up on Greg's transport, on their way to a second chance at life and love. So I went back to Louisiana a few weeks later to find out more about the one thing (or person, I should say) all of them had in common, including my own Albie: Keri Bullock Toth, a four-foot-ten-inch dynamo in her late thirties whose orbit each of these pooches had the good fortune to fall into.

As I stand talking with Dr. Bari Haas in an examination room at her Alexandria area clinic one day, Keri comes in with two terrier mix puppies under her arms. In addition to the endless hours she devotes to rescue, she works full-time here as a vet tech. The pups are about three months old and were dropped off by a woman who'd been given Keri's name by a local pet supply store. Months earlier, the same woman called Keri and told her a dog had been hit by a car and had limped into her yard. Could Keri help? When the injured dog was brought to the clinic, Keri was suspicious — she has uncanny instincts about dogs and about people with dogs. When pressed, the woman admitted the dog was actually hers and it was often left free to roam. The ploy was to try and get veterinary care paid for by the Humane Society of Central Louisiana by pretending it was a stray found by a Good Samaritan. Keri has seen so much of this, and worse, that she often simply shrugs as if to say, "People. What can you do?"

Now, the same woman had dumped the two terrier mix puppies, since named Zinnia and Magnolia, with Keri. Both are soaking wet when Keri places them on the examining room table because the woman bathed them hastily before bringing them in. Keri parts the fur for me to see. Both are covered with fleas. Fleas, like ticks, feed on blood, and a bad infestation can result in anemia and death.

It's clear the dogs need help, *fast*. Dr. Haas immediately administers an oral

medication, Capstar, that will cause the fleas to die and drop off within about fifteen minutes. Keri bathes the pups again and returns to show me the bloody water that has rinsed off them in the small tub. When I see Zinnia and Magnolia the next day, I'm amazed at the transformation. They hardly look like the scraggly, flea-infested puppies I saw the day before. Instead, they are fluffy and as cute as can be and ready to melt the heart of a northern adopter.

But Keri is dismayed because the woman who surrendered them informed her she's keeping a third puppy because her grand-daughter has fallen in love with it. They've already bought a doghouse and a chain, the woman said, two signs the dog will be consigned to living most of its life tethered to a post in the yard. This family has a poor track record of caring for dogs, and Keri isn't going stand by and watch another dog suffer in their care. This puppy stands a better chance of a good life through adoption so Keri hatches a plan to persuade them to surrender the third pup. She sends a text suggesting the first two are showing signs of illness (given their flea infestation, this is defensible if exaggerated) and it's likely the third is also ill and will need costly treatment. Hours later, while Keri, Greta Jones, and I are on our way to a foster home to pick up fifteen dogs to be spayed and neutered, Keri suddenly erupts in a cry of joy. Her ruse worked. She has a text saying the family wants to surrender the third puppy, since named Tulip. From experience, Keri knows these three cuties will be adopted quickly; they're young and they're adorable.

Though Keri and her organization will rescue any kind of dog, many rescue organizations, and rescuers, faced with the over-

whelming magnitude of the problem —
there are thousands upon thousands of dogs
in need of rescue — focus on a particular
breed or type of dog. They may rescue
shepherds or Akitas or Labs, or they may
focus on small shaggy dogs, as Houston
Shaggy Dog Rescue does, or larger long-
haired breeds as Tennessee-based Big
Shaggy Dog Rescue does. Keri does, however, occasionally say no to a dog in need.
Her criteria are more subjective and center
exclusively on temperament and adoptability. If she thinks a dog can be successfully placed, she'll take it under her wing. If
the dog is sick, and many are, the question
is *how sick* and whether she has the resources to nurse it back to health. It's not
uncommon for rescue organizations to
spend more on veterinary care than they
will collect in adoption fees. That's one
reason why so many involved in rescue work
are spending from their own pockets or running up debts, as Keri has, at veterinary
clinics.

I soon learn that anyone involved with
animals within a hundred miles of Alexandria — veterinarians, shelter personnel,
pet store staff, dog salon owners, and animal
welfare advocates — knows Keri Toth. And
there are thousands of people up north with

rescue dogs with Keri's fingerprints on them, many of whom know her by name. Over the past ten years or so, Keri has placed several thousand dogs from Louisiana in northern homes. In recent years, she's been placing six to seven hundred a year — so many that in late 2012, Greg added Alexandria to his route to serve her and her organization.

I am particularly interested in Keri because she, like Greg, was instrumental in bringing Albie to us. I want to know what makes her tick and how she manages to work full-time as a vet tech and rescue hundreds of dogs a year all while raising four children. She tells me she's missed a lot of their growing up because of her commitment to rescue and it has sometimes strained her marriage to the breaking point, but she has persevered.

The daughter of a Baptist preacher, Keri has lived in Louisiana almost her entire life. Her accent, to my northern ears at least, recalls Dolly Parton. Keri's first memory of rescue goes back to third grade, when she saved a lizard from her cat's mouth.

"My dad was yelling at me to get ready for church," she tells me, "so I put it in a little container and put rubbing alcohol on the lizard, where the cat had made bite marks. That killed the lizard, but it was my first effort at rescue."

A year later, when she was eight, Keri lost her cat, Bluejean, whom she found dead by the church where her father preached.

"He finally admitted he had stepped on her by accident," Keri recalls, "and he felt terrible." She composed a little ode, which she recalls precisely: "On top of old Blue, all covered with flies, there sat old Keri, crying out her eyes." The experience, she says, "got me started in forever saving animals."

While a student at the University of Louisiana at Monroe, Keri started volunteering at the Monroe Humane Society. When she moved to Alexandria in 2003, she started the Humane Society of Central Louisiana. In the fall of 2004, through a long series of connections, she began working as a volunteer adoption coordinator for Labs4rescue. She went to the Alexandria shelter the next week and pulled four Lab mixes. She's been finding homes for dogs through Labs4rescue and other organizations ever since.

Although Keri works full-time as a vet tech for Dr. Haas, it's hard to know where her work there ends and her rescue work begins. Dr. Haas is deeply engaged in Keri's mission and her day too is a mixture of treating people's pets and providing medical care to Keri's dogs.[17]

Keri's days are filled with a blizzard of text messages, emails, and phone calls related to dogs in need and dogs being adopted. She's a woman under constant siege and also has to deal with a lot of "crazies," as she calls them, people such as the woman with the two terrier mix puppies claiming to have found an injured dog when, in fact, it's her dog and she's hoping to scam some free veterinary care.

"We'll pay for the care," says Keri, "but they have to surrender the dog." Then Keri can ensure it gets placed in a home where it will be loved and properly cared for. One woman called Keri insisting she pay for her dog's cancer care, even though the woman was well aware that she was calling an animal rescue/adoption organization while having no intention of giving up the dog. "I explained that we are here trying to solve the animal overpopulation problem, but she was indignant that I was going to let her

17. It should be noted Keri doesn't just rescue dogs; she also rescues many cats, which are all adopted out locally, after being spayed or neutered. But her work with Greg is for the dogs.

dog die," says Keri. "We get a lot of crazy calls [like that]."

One of her biggest challenges is similar to the one Greg faced when it became apparent we were going to have a very full load: Where do you put all the dogs you rescue?

At any given time, Keri will be fostering a dozen or more at her home in Deville (she and her husband, Phillip, live on twenty-four acres), Greta Jones will have some at her house, others will be spread out — one, two, or three at a time — at other foster homes in the area with whomever Keri can persuade to take in a dog or two for a few weeks. Some are on "hold" at the shelters in Alexandria or Pineville, meaning someone has identified the dog as one he or she intends to adopt or to find a home for. (Pineville has the only other nearby shelter with a roof; there's an outdoor holding pen for strays in Colfax, about half an hour north). Some are boarded at Dr. Haas's clinic. Finding temporary places for dogs is one of Keri's constant challenges and biggest headaches, an ever-shifting puzzle as more dogs are rescued and brought to Keri and others sent on their way with Greg.

Fostering a dozen may seem like borderline hoarding, but in Keri's case it's not. "If the dogs don't leave," says Keri, "that's hoarding." She simply keeps them temporarily until she can find permanent or foster homes for them. That said, hoarding, a form of mental illness, is something of an occupational hazard in rescue circles; it's a slippery slope between wanting to save every animal and being unable or unwilling to let any of them go.

One day, after she'd worked a full day, Keri, Greta, and I drive in Greta's van about a half hour to Prospect, Louisiana, in Grant Parish, about twenty minutes from Pineville. Keri has a woman in Prospect, Diana, a single mom, who fosters for her. On the way Keri admits she has concerns, though. Diana takes in so many dogs from people in the area, including the Grant Parish sheriff's department because their holding pen in Colfax is so small, that Keri fears she may be a borderline hoarder, and she's concerned about the conditions of the kennels at Diana's.

We're going to pick up fifteen dogs to bring them back to the Haas Animal Hospital for the night. Tomorrow morning, a van from SpayNation, a low-cost spay and neuter organization based ninety miles south in Lafayette, is going to take the dogs for their surgery. They'll spend the night in

Lafayette and be returned to Pineville the next day.

When we arrive at Diana's and the usual barking erupts, I see why Keri is concerned. There's a very large fenced yard with about a half-dozen dogs running around and in one corner a few pens floored with wooden pallets into which a few small doghouses have been placed. As Keri points out, the dog waste may fall or be washed through the spaces in the pallets, but underneath, it's basically a smelly, raw sewer. And there's little shelter from the weather.

Toward the far back of the property is another enclosure where dogs are living. All together, there appear to be at least two-dozen dogs here, maybe more. Diana tells me she's had more than forty at times. Some of these are dogs Keri has asked Diana to foster, but since roles often get blurred in the fluid world of rescue work, Keri has also assumed responsibility for trying to adopt out many of the other dogs Diana has taken in too.

Hoarding is a complex psychological phenomenon whether people hoard things or animals. Animal hoarders often truly believe they are saving animals from a worse fate and that they are doing right by those in their care. And they may slip into hoarding without even realizing it. While being unable to let go of the animals taken in is indicative of hoarding, so is taking in more animals than you can reasonably care of properly. That's why Keri thinks Diana may fall somewhere along the hoarding spectrum — she simply doesn't have the resources or time to care for all the dogs in the way they need and deserve.

The roundup of the fifteen dogs headed to SpayNation is loud and chaotic. Many of them push through the kennel doors as soon as they're opened and are running willy-nilly around the yard. Keri and Diana grab them and lift them, some quite large, over the four-foot high fence to Greta and me to be put in kennels in the van. Some are scared and could snap at us, so I keep a careful eye out for these and try to let Greta, who is far more experienced than me, handle them. As I learned when we boarded poor Teddy in Alexandria a few weeks ago, you have to be on your guard for a dog that may try and bite. Luckily, none of us are bitten, but by the time the dogs are loaded, we're drenched with sweat and have poop smeared all over our shirts and pants. If you're always moving a lot of dogs around, especially puppies, it comes with the territory.

As we head back to Pineville, Keri ponders the quandary about Diana. Conditions at Diana's are far from ideal for the dogs, but unfortunately, Keri's options are limited. Every dog she can foster *somewhere* is a dog that isn't being euthanized elsewhere. So she sometimes accepts less-than-ideal circumstances because the alternatives are worse. Yet, if she can't get the dogs at Diana's spayed, neutered, and vaccinated, and ensure that they are fully healthy — all of which are crucial to move them along toward adoption — why leave them there? One thing is certain: when the dogs return from SpayNation with fresh surgical wounds and stitches that will need proper care, she does not want them to go back into the unsanitary living quarters at Diana's. She's determined to have another place for all fifteen by the time they get back from Lafayette and she has about thirty-six hours to come up with a plan.

Problem solving on the fly is a constant in Keri's life. If there's a dog in distress, she doesn't think, *Do I have a place for this dog?* Her heart, not her head is her guide. She acts, takes the poor creature in, and crosses the next bridge when she comes to it. Move this dog here today even if she doesn't know where he'll go tomorrow. If she needed to have a complete plan from the outset she might never save a dog. It's not about logic; it's about love.

With the clock ticking, Keri and Greta ruminate about what to do. Greta wonders if they should buy a few ten-by-ten-foot temporary kennel runs and set them up in Sara Kelly's backyard — Sara Kelly is the physician whose rescue organization, the Central Louisiana (CenLa) Alliance for Animals, is merging with Keri's soon. It was Sara who fostered Trudy, the deaf and blind Catahoula mix, and Popcorn, and her home is where they bonded. But Sara lives in a quiet suburban subdivision, where the neighbors are already concerned about how many dogs she's fostering. A few other names are tossed out: What about the Smiths? Could they board a few more at Dr. Haas's? How many more could Keri and Greta take to their own homes for temporary lodging?

It's nearing 9:00 p.m. as we return to Pineville, so Keri's going to have to figure it out tomorrow. For now, she has to get the fifteen dogs dewormed, vaccinated, given their heartworm preventative, bathed, and settled in for the night at the clinic. She's expected home in an hour, but it's well after midnight before she stumbles into bed.

133

Keri is still up bright and early the next morning at 4:30 a.m. so she can meet the SpayNation people at the clinic and help them load the dogs. Then she's going to start her regular workday while trying to serve as the adoption coordinator for dozens of dogs cleared for transport and listed on the Labs4rescue and Mutts4rescue websites, which means reviewing applications, arranging home visits, and getting all the paperwork together so she can put them on Greg's truck in the near future. And in preparation for their first family vacation in years, which begins in a few days, she needs to make sure all her own animals and the fosters in her direct care will be attended to while she's away. If it weren't for this kind of exhausting dedication, dogs such as Jupee and Pam, Seth and Salyna, Trudy and Popcorn and T-Bone and all the others would never have made it north, not to mention Albie.

Like the countless people up north who have adopted dogs with Keri's help, I had no idea of the investment in time, money, and emotion that goes into her work. She transforms lives, canine and human, yet to those most impacted by her work, she's nearly invisible, just a name, an email address, and a phone number. There are no awards or public recognition, just the occasional thank-you note. But for countless dogs Greg drives north to their forever homes, and for their new families, Keri couldn't be more important.

Ever since we adopted Albie, I've wondered: Why are so many rescued dogs from the South? There are, to be sure, shelter dogs up north in need of homes. Dogs are abused and discarded by their owners north of the Mason–Dixon line too.

But the vast majority of rescued dogs come from southern states such as Louisiana, Mississippi, Tennessee, and others. How come? There are some simple answers I already touched upon, such as a general lack of spaying and neutering, which explodes the canine population well beyond the capacity of local communities to find homes for them all. But why is spaying and neutering common practice in some parts of the country and not others? Why are so many southern dogs left to wander and breed freely? Why are unwanted litters of puppies wrapped in garbage bags and thrown in Dumpsters or tossed out of moving vehicles onto roadways or left in plastic tubs at a veterinarian's clinic? Why are dogs that won't hunt simply abandoned deep in the woods?

I got an unexpected hint at the answer when I learned that Louisiana Governor Bobby Jindal had recently vetoed a bill passed by the state legislature and backed by animal welfare advocates that would have prohibited dogs from riding in the back of open pickup trucks unless safely confined in a kennel secured to the truck . . . but only on highways where the speed limit was seventy-five mph. Why such specific circumstances for this law? Louisiana is filled with sportsmen who are accompanied by dogs in their pickup trucks, so animal welfare advocates, being realistic, aimed only for a prohibition on unsecured dogs on high-speed interstates. The dangers of transport in the back of an open pickup are obvious: not only can a dog that jumps or is jarred loose from the back of a pickup be injured or killed, but it could endanger other drivers and their passengers too. Imagine the chaos that would follow a dog flying out of the back of a pickup with cars and trucks traveling behind at seventy-five or eighty mph.

But opponents of the bill saw their "way of life" threatened by such a measure. What I realized is that the root of many of the problems afflicting so many dogs here is social and cultural; as noted earlier, dogs are viewed by many simply as property, and they don't want anyone, especially government, telling them what they can or cannot do with their property. That goes for spay and neuter laws too.

Indeed, in his veto statement, Governor Jindal wrote, "Animal cruelty is explicitly prohibited by current law, and I trust that our citizens can care for their pets without the nanny state intervening to dictate how a dog is secured in the bed of a pickup." In short, the reasons for the surfeit of southern dogs are social, cultural, and political.

Animal cruelty may be prohibited by law, but public irresponsibility when it comes to animals is widespread in Louisiana. In an op-ed column in New Orleans's major newspaper *The Times-Picayune* following the governor's veto, Ken Levy, a law professor at Louisiana State University, wrote, "Louisiana is not exactly known for its responsible, compassionate treatment of animals. Unfortunately, Gov. Bobby Jindal . . . seems intent on keeping it this way. Despite massive efforts to educate pet owners and breeders, Louisiana boasts one of the lowest spay/neuter rates and therefore one of the highest pet overpopulation rates in the nation. As a result, every year, tens of thousands of cats and dogs are herded into local shelters and euthanized."[18]

Data keeping in the thousands of public shelters across the United States varies greatly and getting reliable, complete state-by-state euthanasia statistics can be next to impossible, making comparisons difficult. Even within states the information is often incomplete, nonexistent, or kept inconsistently. Anecdotally, though, it's clear the overpopulation problem is far more acute in southern states.

For example, the Alexandria shelter, where Albie spent several months and where Keri pulls many dogs, serves Rapides and Grant Parishes, which have a combined population of 155,000 people. In 2013, it took in 3,499 dogs, of which 87 percent (3,041) were euthanized, according to official data provided by the city.

By comparison, the state of New Jersey has a population of nearly nine million people, fifty-eight times that of Rapides and

18. According to the Humane Society of the United States more than ninety thousand dogs and cats are euthanized annually in Louisiana, a number that doesn't include uncounted animals killed or neglected to death by their owners, or those who die before ever reaching a shelter.

Grant Parishes. Yet, according to the New Jersey Department of Health, its twenty-one county shelters impounded a total 33,538 dogs in 2013, just ten times the number impounded in Alexandria, of which only 13 percent, 4,509, were put down. One reason for this disparity is that with such a large population, there are many more potential adopters in highly populated states such as New Jersey and far fewer dogs impounded relative to the size of the population.

And it's not just Louisiana. Maddie's Fund, a California-based family foundation devoted to the well-being of companion animals, has assembled dog impoundment and euthanasia data from various states and counties around the country. In Mobile County, Alabama, in 2012, for example, nearly nine thousand dogs were taken into shelters with approximately four thousand euthanized (44 percent), almost as many as were euthanized in the entire state of New Jersey in 2013. Yet, Mobile County has a population of roughly four hundred thousand people, less than 5 percent of the population of New Jersey. In Monroe County, Tennessee, population forty-five thousand, nearly three thousand dogs were taken in at the shelter in 2012, one for every fifteen people, and roughly one thousand were euthanized. Again, a single county with a population one–two hundredth the size of New Jersey's took in about one-tenth the number of dogs and euthanized almost a quarter the number. This would be like New Jersey shelters taking in six hundred thousand dogs and euthanizing two hundred thousand of them.

Even more shocking perhaps is the estimated number of stray dogs living on the streets of Houston, one of the nation's largest cities. The city and rescue groups agree it's about 1.2 million. No northern city has a canine overpopulation problem anywhere near that scale. The entire city of New York (with a human population of eight million) took in just over fifteen thousand dogs in 2012. Detroit has been estimated to have a stray dog population of fifty thousand, though a 2014 study put the number as low as three thousand.

There are other nonsouthern states where the problem is serious, though still not as serious by the numbers as in the South. For example, in 2012, in four northern California counties (Alameda, Contra Costa, San Francisco, and Santa Clara) with a combined population of 5.3 million people, a little more than half the population of New

Jersey, the shelters took in about forty thousand dogs and euthanized about 25 percent. A little over sixty thousand dogs were taken into Maricopa, Arizona, shelters in 2012 and about one-third were euthanized. The county includes the Phoenix metropolitan area and has a population around four million, one of the most populous counties in the United States.

Yes, there are dogs in need of homes everywhere, and the overpopulation problem isn't confined to the South, but the problem is especially critical there.

"There's a lack of value placed on pets here," Dr. Haas tells me during a conversation at her clinic during which she chooses her words carefully. "I don't want to say ignorance, but there's a lack of knowledge about responsible pet ownership. It has changed since I came to this area to practice in 1988. Back then you could go to the shelter and get a dog for five dollars and a cat for three with no background check and no requirement that the animal be spayed or neutered. As the area has grown and people have come from other parts of the country, values have started to shift. But for a lot of people, if they have a sick animal, they'd just as soon spend fifteen cents on a bullet than take it to the vet. The animal is an object that's disposable.

"These attitudes get passed down generation to generation, and isn't just animals," adds Dr. Haas. "I have clients who stopped coming here because of Mr. Robin." Mr. Robin, the vet tech, is African American. "They don't even want him to touch their animals. If you can't respect people who are different from you, you won't respect animals. It's very hard to change a culture, even a culture of pet ownership. I have a client who has no qualms about buying a female dog to breed it with his male so he can get one male puppy to keep. He kills the other pups and sells the mother. As the male puppy ages, he'll do the same thing again. This is the mentality of many people here."

Keri and Dr. Haas agree the only thing that can change the culture is education. Dr. Haas sees that as part of her mission: to educate clients one at a time about responsible pet ownership.

"If I don't teach them, how can I expect them to be responsible pet owners?" she asks. "It's a one-person-at-a-time effort. I see people coming in with their pets who used to come in with their parents as children, and now they are teaching their own children how to be responsible. It takes time, generations, to change deep-seated attitudes."

For Keri's part, she wants to find the time to develop a program she calls C.A.R.E. (Caring for Animals Responsibly through Education), modeled on the drug education program D.A.R.E. (Drug Abuse Resistance Education). She envisions partnering with local sheriffs' departments, which have animal control jurisdiction, to bring programs into the schools to teach children about responsible pet ownership.[19]

"We have to change the culture," she says.

19. Some in rescue believe that the term "animal control" is itself a problem in shaping the mission and attitudes of those in charge of shelters. The public shelters I visited in Louisiana are referred to as "animal control" facilities and many bear names that identify them that way, such as the City of Alexandria Animal Control and Lafayette Parish Animal Control. The linguistic emphasis is on control, not care. They are not called animal "welfare" or animal "protection" facilities, for example. No one is suggesting that simply changing the name would result in major changes, but that the word *control* reflects a mission and mindset that doesn't necessarily have animal welfare at its core.

"Animals have feelings, just as we do. We need to teach children that they feel hurt, pain, hunger, and love; they are not just a piece of property."

She envisions a program where the kids "graduate" and earn a certificate, something to instill pride and life lessons they may forget in their adolescent years but to which they will return as adults. "You can't just crucify; you have edify," she says. "And when you do, those people will become your best allies.

"Right now we're just so focused on getting as many dogs out, we haven't been able to focus on the education part," adds Keri. Hopefully, that will change once she has finalized the merger with Sara Kelly's CenLa Alliance for Animals. Until then, she and everyone else involved in rescue in Louisiana is on a hamster wheel trying to save as many dogs as they can.

Later in the day, Keri, Greta, and I set out again for rural Grant Parish. Only twenty thousand people live here and household trash disposal is rudimentary. At dozens of locations around the parish, sometimes down remote dirt roads, sometimes by the side of main roads, there are clusters of small Dumpsters where residents throw

144

their trash. Nothing is sorted: newspapers, plastics, household chemicals, paints, garbage, and organic material — it's all disposed of together. Stray dogs and cats often scavenge at these sites; too often puppies and kittens, dead or alive, are thrown into them too. We're going to see if there are any animals in need of rescue.

As we drive, I ask Keri about her faith. I'm curious to know if her rescue work is faith driven in any way. Though her father was a Southern Baptist preacher, Keri considers herself a nondenominational person of faith.

"Rescue work is degrading work in a way," she says, referring to spending long hours in poop-smeared clothes and walking through redolent dumpsites in search of dogs and cats. "But in Genesis it says we were put here to take care of the animals. Why did God create Adam? To take care of the animals. This is part of my calling."

As we step out of the car at the first of four Dumpster sites we're going to check for strays, the stench of fish rotting in the hot Louisiana sun is thick. Keri already has her hands full with all the dogs at Diana's, but in her heart, there's always room for more. She knows strays forage at these sites, and she can't bear the thought of ignoring them. At every site, there are dead fish dumped on the ground, some still intact, some nearly rotted away. Keri surmises local fishermen leave them for the dogs and cats they know scavenge the areas.

As Keri wanders into the brush, meowing and clicking her tongue, hoping to lure shy animals out from the underbrush, Greta and I peer into each Dumpster to see if there are any dogs or cats inside. We find nothing and begin to wander into some of the nearby brush ourselves when I ask a question I immediately regret.

"Are there snakes?"

"Oh, for sure," answers Greta. "Keep an eye out. There are rattle-snakes, copper-heads, and coral snakes."

Coral snakes? I remember reading they are one of the most venomous snakes found in North America. Now, instead of scanning the brush forty yards away for stray dogs, I'm scanning the grass four feet in front my shoes for snakes.

Finding nothing at the first site — no dogs, no cats, no snakes — we move on. At the second, there are signs of dogs living nearby. Someone has placed a small dog bed in the underbrush and a bowl filled with water. The sun-bleached spine of a long-dead unidentified animal, about two feet

146

long, sits nearby.

Though Keri says they almost always find dogs and cats during their Dumpster dives, today we strike out. I'm not sure if that's a bad thing or a good thing. Truth be told, I found myself peering into about two-dozen Dumpsters with trepidation, half hoping we might be able to rescue a distressed dog, half hoping we'd find nothing because I wasn't sure I could bear the sight.

After our Dumpster foray, we head for the Grant Parish dog pound in Colfax. Strays picked up by one of the two parish animal control officers are brought here. The facility — if one can call it that — isn't even a shelter: it's two small open-air pens with concrete floors enclosed by chain-link fencing. The only protection from the weather is a couple of portable kennels and an igloo-shaped play structure. The floor of the pen on the left has recently been hosed down, but the one on the right is filthy. There are about two-dozen dogs in all, with males and females, puppies and older dogs mixed together, including five black Lab puppies about ten weeks old. As I gaze around the dismal area, it's clear to me infection control here would be impossible, and puppies tend to carry infectious diseases, such as parvovirus and distemper. Parvovirus, or parvo for short, is an infectious disease spread through direct or indirect contact with feces. It's common in puppies, especially those living in close, dirty conditions like this. Distemper is a highly contagious viral airborne disease that affects the gastrointestinal tract, respiratory tract, brain, and spinal cord. Both are easily preventable with vaccines but can be deadly if contracted and left untreated.[20] Ideally you'd segregate the puppies and vaccinate them. But there's no medical treatment here, unless Keri and Greta do it themselves. And unspayed females and unneutered males aren't segregated either. This is about as rudimentary as shelters get.

Keri and Greta tell me the left pen is vastly improved from their last visit; then there were puppies with parvo (the signs are obvious, including bloody diarrhea and vomiting) mixed with healthy dogs and filth everywhere. That the floor has at least been washed with a high-pressure hose is a small victory.

Keri has phoned ahead, and one of the two Grant Parish animal control officers,

20. Parvovirus and distemper cannot infect humans.

148

Bert, meets us there and I learn the facility is monitored by the officers but not staffed. Bert seems friendly and well-meaning, and Keri and Greta have been working to encourage modest improvements in how the dogs are cared for. The problem is Bert is manifestly overweight and the other officer is disabled. So neither is really up to the physical work required to keep pens clean and manage the dogs.

As we chat, Keri's sixth sense tells her something is amiss in the one small portable kennel in the filthy pen, and she walks along the fence to get a better view. Upon discovering there's a dead dog inside, she tells Bert, who takes a look and promises to take care of it.

My sense is she's not at all surprised about the dead dog. Keri has seen enough animal suffering and death to sometimes be matter-of-fact about it, as she is now, though she is often on the verge of tears when she sees an animal in distress. Thankfully, I can't see inside the kennel from where I'm standing and I choose not to look. I'm still taken aback by the filth and primitiveness of the whole facility. It seems as though we've stumbled into a poverty-stricken Third World village.

Another of the dogs appears to have motor oil on its back. "The redneck way of treating mange," says Keri.

In the left pen, Greta spots a dog she is sure is a sister to one of her fosters, Handley, a beagle mix. The age, coloring, gait, and overall appearance are nearly identical and Handley was also a stray found in this area.

Any dog not claimed by its owner here will be sent to the Alexandria shelter to be put down, so Keri and Greta take as many dogs that appear adoptable as they can from the Colfax pound. They tell Bert they'll be back the next day to get the dog that appears to be Handley's sister (which Greta will foster) and one other; if Keri weren't leaving on vacation, there are half a dozen she'd pull; take to Dr. Haas's clinic to be dewormed, vaccinated, and started on heartworm preventive; and take home until she could find foster homes. She also tells Bert she'll be bringing enough vaccines to begin treating all the dogs. Since none have health records, it's impossible to know if any have ever been inoculated against the common canine viruses and rabies.

As we drive away Keri and Greta also make a plan to return with a large, flat shovel to clear the filth from the right pen, so they can hose it down and disinfect it as best they can. They also noted one of the females, a basset hound–rat terrier mix, was very pregnant, so they will buy some cedar chips at a pet supply so the mama at least has a soft place to deliver her pups. It's not as if they don't have a million other things to do, but this is how they roll: to see a problem involving desperate dogs is to do something about it. It's as if they are compelled to act by some invisible force. They get nothing in return but the satisfaction of relieving a tiny piece of suffering in a large ocean of it. I've never seen two more selfless people at work.

On the drive back toward Pineville, Keri announces she's resolved the quandary about the fifteen dogs returning in the morning from SpayNation. It's not a perfect solution but it'll work for the time being. She's found a new foster for two, she and Greta will each take one and two will be boarded at Dr. Haas's clinic. The other nine will go back to Diana's, but Keri and Greta will spend a few hours cleaning up the pens first. When Keri gets back from vacation, they have a more ambitious plan for Diana's: they are going to relocate the pens to a spot on the property with better drainage and have concrete floors poured (donated hopefully) because they can be cleaned and disinfected; the wooden pallets currently being used cannot.

"We can break the kennels down in three or four hours," Greta tells me. "We know how to do it." The word *tireless* comes to mind. I'm simply in awe of the way Keri and Greta constantly seem to take on more and more, and I'm humbled too. It's far more than I'd ever be able to do, even though I've now seen firsthand the suffering of so many dogs here. I know they get exhausted and that the work can be so sad and depressing it takes a huge emotional toll too, but their reservoir of energy and resilience seems infinite. I can only marvel at it.

When you do the work Keri and Greta do, nothing surprises you anymore. The next day, they learn from Bert that, during the night, three puppies, presumably alive, were tossed over the fence at the Colfax pound into one of the pens. When Bert arrived for the morning check, all were dead. And a few days later, all of the black Lab puppies we'd seen there were also dead, victims of parvo. Such is the plight of countless dogs in Louisiana.

While I was back in Alexandria, Keri arranged for me to spend a day with Sara Kelly, with whom she is joining forces. She thought it would give me a broader view of the rescue work being done in central Louisiana. Historically, Sara's organization, the CenLa Alliance for Animals (CAFA), wasn't a rescue organization. Though it does limited rescue work now, the focus is on improving animal welfare through education, public awareness, and spay and neuter programs. Keri's Humane Society of Central Louisiana is a rescue organization pure and simple. The merged organizations will do both, giving Keri a platform for the education programs she knows are the only way rescue will cease to be an endless cycle that fails to address the underlying problem, and expanding CAFA's mission to formally include rescue.

Because she's constantly moving dogs around, and has two young daughters, Sydney, age four, and Campbell, age six, it almost goes without saying that Sara drives a large SUV with kennels in the back. Our first stop is going to be a suburban home near Alexandria, where Sara has someone fostering two heeler mix puppies that need vaccinations she will administer.

Sara, trim, fit, and in her early forties, was raised near Dallas, graduated from the

University of Texas, and received her medical training in Iowa. Her specialty is emergency medicine. Her husband, Dan Oas, an orthopedic trauma surgeon, hails from Minnesota. In addition to serving as CAFA's president and being a mom, she owns an urgent care center where she works, manages investment properties in Hawaii, and is developing a line of pet toys. She's driven, organized, and determined, all useful traits when you multitask the way she does. She describes herself as a type A personality.

I tell Sara I was startled by a statistic on the CAFA website: one unspayed female dog and one unneutered male and their unspayed and unneutered offspring can produce sixty-seven thousand puppies in six years.

She explains how they're trying to stop the rapidly spreading problem of overbreeding and overpopulation. "We partner with local vets to provide financial assistance to low income families so they can spay and neuter their pets and have them vaccinated," Sara says. "This helps reduce euthanasia rates and the spread of preventable disease."

Though CAFA, which Sara revitalized over the past couple of years, didn't have rescue as part of its mission, in early 2013, she started pulling dogs and cats from the

Alexandria shelter, the shelter where Albie spent four months. She sought Keri's help placing the animals in forever homes. In her first year, CAFA facilitated six hundred rescues, mostly transfers to other rescue organizations doing direct adoptions, but some direct adoptions also, which Keri managed. For example, in 2014, CAFA started sending dogs to the Empty Shelter Project, a no-kill facility in Virginia that adopts them out. Sara and others meet staff from the project in Atlanta, where the dogs are transferred to vehicles that will take them to Virginia. One of the huge benefits for CAFA is that the Empty Shelter Project accepts healthy, unvaccinated dogs and unaltered dogs, bearing the costs of vaccinations and spaying and neutering.

"Keri and I hope the merger of our organizations will allow us to have a greater impact," Sara tells me. "We have tremendous need here. We could fill Greg's truck every trip if we had the resources to get the work done."

When we arrive where the two female heeler mix puppies are, no one is home and Sara's unable to get the keyless entry system to work. But we see the puppies in the yard through the fence. As puppies are wont to

155

do, as soon as they see us, they can't run fast enough to get to where we are standing. With the confident hand of an experienced physician, Sara reaches over and grabs the first puppy by the scruff of the neck with one hand. With the other, she reaches into a small bag with the vaccines, pops the tip of a syringe off with her teeth, and in a matter of seconds, the first puppy has received his third set of vaccines. She repeats the process with the second puppy. Now that they've had their third set of vaccines, the puppies can go on Greg's transport as soon as adopting families, or a foster, can be found.

We're back in the car within minutes, heading to a local veterinary clinic where two puppies Sara pulled from the Alexandria shelter are being treated for parvo. As we drive, Sara's cell phone rings constantly: calls from her urgent care center, calls about dogs, calls about picking up the kids from school later in the day. Like Keri and Greta, Sara is a woman of action, and I'm beginning to get the sense that this is the way life in rescue is for everyone: long hours, endless demands, and equally endless energy.

"I don't have time to do everything I do, but I do it anyway," she says.

Sara's love of animals began as a child, when she learned to ride horses, a skill she honed in competitions growing up.

"I started rescuing barn cats where I kept my horse as a kid," she tells me. "And I've always had an affinity for the sick and the injured, which is why I became a doctor." During her residency in Tulsa, she spent her off hours volunteering for a feral cat spay and neuter program that would trap, neuter, and release or adopt stray cats in the area.

Even with the merger of Sara's organization and Keri's, the challenges will remain the same. Neither organization has much in the way of financial nor human resources — Sara, Keri, and Greta will be the nucleus — and finding local foster homes will continue to be a chronic problem.

"We have some people who will take entire litters until they are old enough to travel," Sara explains, "but typically people are only willing to take one or two at a time and will foster only once or twice."

As we pull up to the veterinary clinic, Sara tells me about Tupak, a pit bull she rescued who is now being fostered by one of the vet techs here. "He was stabbed in the eye," she tells me, "and we had to remove it. He was abandoned and alone. But he's as sweet as

they come, and now he's a registered therapy dog."

You hear countless stories like this when
you spend time with rescue people; it's
remarkable how many dogs have suffered so
much at the hands of humans but still are
ready to love and trust us.

Inside the clinic we first visit Jake, an
eight-week-old black Lab mix who has signs
of parvo. Sara explains they don't test for
parvo; it's so common in the area, they
simply treat on the assumption the dog has
the disease if it displays any symptoms at
all, such as loose stools. Jake has another
problem causing him to limp, an abscess on
one of his rear legs. As Sara lifts him up,
blood and pus ooze from his hindquarters.

The second puppy, which has no name, is
a ten-week-old Lab mix, the only survivor
from a litter of eight pulled from the Alexandria shelter. The others had parvo, and
possibly distemper, and died from dehydra-
tion caused by diarrhea. Sara is fostering
the mother at home and using an IV to keep
the puppy hydrated. For so many of these
poor pups, the road to a forever home is a
very long one, if they are even lucky enough
to survive.

Our next stop is the Alexandria shelter, a

place I've wondered about ever since we adopted Albie. Albie lived here for several months before coming to us and was fortunate to have made it out alive. The euthanasia rate here is close to 90 percent. Sara is a regular visitor here and the shelter director, Henry Wimbley, allows her to vaccinate dogs she has identified as ones she wants to pull and adopt out. Now she's arranged to let me walk through the shelter with her and to see where Albie was before he was saved.

There's nothing foreboding about the facility, a one-story, mostly brick structure in a light industrial area, with a small lobby and a receptionist's window. After a perfunctory greeting, Mr. Wimbley allows us to walk around freely, though he makes sure Sara doesn't take me to see the crematorium. I presume the thinking is, "out of sight, out of mind."

Every shelter has one thing in common: barking dogs. The stress of working under such conditions must be enormous. As we walk by the pens — cages really — most dogs, desperate for contact with anyone, leap at the bars or push their noses as far forward as they can, each seemingly competing for attention. Place your hand or finger nearby, and they are desperate for a human touch. Some will lie quietly, as if they've been through this a million times, and have surrendered all hope, which is equally devastating to see.

A public animal shelter is an inherently dispiriting place. The presence of a staff member or passerby is virtually the only stimulation the dogs get unless there are volunteers to walk them occasionally; their kennels or cages are bare concrete or wire mesh fenced enclosures. Almost uniformly among the shelters I visited, there are few toys, nothing to chew on, and nothing to do. For some, the tedium gets to be too much and they pace or run around in circles, as caged animals often do at zoos.

At Alexandria, some kennels are outdoors, under a roof but open on the sides. Others are inside. As we walk through, Sara checks on dogs she has identified for rescue by CAFA, reading the notations on the cards that are posted on each kennel, checking for dates of last vaccines. In some cases, she opens the door and administers a vaccine. She also looks at the cards of dogs she may want to pull to see when they were brought in, any remarks written by shelter staff, and any notations related to the dogs' statuses. Sometimes dogs have been seized following complaints and are awaiting a court ruling on whether they can be returned to the owner. In others, the dog has been identified as a biter.

To my untrained eye, the shelter appears relatively clean, but as I learn from Sara, clean and sanitary are not the same thing.

"This shelter is a hot zone for parvo and distemper," she tells me. "If you know a dog is sick, it should be isolated, and puppies should always be separated from the rest of the shelter population. If a puppy has disease symptoms, it shouldn't share a kennel with any other puppy for three months. Workers should be decontaminated as they move from one section of the shelter to another because some are airborne diseases easily carried on workers' boots, for example. Parvo can live in walls and hosing them down may make the place look cleaner but it's not preventing the spread of disease. Viral particles are widely shared throughout the shelter. Everything here is intermingled."

In 2005, Keri Toth was part of a team with the Protective Animal Welfare Society, the predecessor organization of Sara's CAFA, that investigated euthanasia practices at the Alexandria shelter. Until recently, county prisoners, known as "trustees," provided manual labor at the shelter, as they do at many shelters in Louisiana, and Keri recorded conversations with trustees who had worked there. According to Keri, they described the dogs being euthanized as held around the neck with a catchpole while the heart stick, a lethal intracardial injection, was administered. Some of those interviewed described scenes in which animals were put in the incinerator alive following failed heart stick administration and crying dogs and cats being drowned in buckets.

Opinions differ, even among those engaged in rescue work in and around Alexandria, about the way the shelter is run, whether enough is being done to lower the euthanasia rate (through a more robust adoption program, for example) and the level of cooperation between rescue organizations and shelter staff. Some think the shelter is doing the best it can under the circumstances in a region with a severe cat and dog overpopulation problem; others think the level of cooperation is grudging and might be nonexistent but for their constant pressure.

The relationship between the shelter and the rescue organizations, at least Keri's and Sara's, seems to be marked by some wariness on both sides. The shelter sees the rescue groups as meddling critics and the rescues see the shelter as resistant to change. Yet there is a level of mutual cooperation necessary if rescue groups are going to save as many dogs as they can and if the shelter is going to be seen by the public as something other than a mere slaughterhouse.

"The philosophy of the shelter, and this is true throughout most of the state, is animal control by any means necessary," Sara tells me. "Mr. Wimbley and I have reached an uneasy truce. He tries to help me and I try not to make his life difficult. The better our relationship is, the better it is for the shelter, for the dogs, and for CAFA. He can help us with our mission, and we can help keep the shelter kill rate down and help improve conditions for the animals there."

Sara realizes being a physician in a small community where she knows the movers and shakers gives her some leverage in effecting change and she uses it. "He knows I can make a fuss, so he has an interest in keeping me happy," she says.

"When I started pulling puppies and kittens from the shelter in 2013, almost all the puppies and kittens were euthanized immediately even though they are the most adoptable," Sara tells me. "The view was that puppies and kittens carry disease and the shelter was not equipped to take care of them. Now, Mr. Wimbley allows me to vaccinate some dogs at the shelter and they vaccinate some themselves. If an animal isn't immediately euthanized, it should be vaccinated and dewormed. Here they wait to see if an animal survives the early days; *then* they might invest in vaccinations and other medications. Sometimes dogs are at the shelter three to ten days and then they decide it might be worth the investment, but by then the dogs have been exposed and it's too late. Parvo and distemper are rampant. We're always playing catch up on vaccines with the dogs."

Sara believes the euthanasia rate of nearly 90 percent is higher than it could be if infection control were better. Some otherwise healthy animals that would be candidates for adoption are becoming ill at the shelter and fall into the category of sick animals that need to be euthanized.

Dwelling on shelter euthanasia statistics, while important, misses a larger point, however. While most would agree the lower the rate the better, whether the euthanasia rate is 50 or 70 or 90 percent, the point is that in Louisiana alone, an estimated ninety thousand dogs and cats are put down each year and many are perfectly healthy, adoptable animals. The euthanasia rate gives you a sense of the scale of the overpopulation problem.

As Sara and I walked through the shelter I couldn't stop thinking about Albie, and it was painful to picture him — our sweet, loving, and trusting Albie, who enjoys nothing more than to lope through the woods — sitting there day after day behind bars on a concrete floor, alone most of the time.

That he survived for four months seemed a miracle when I considered the odds. The receptionist looked up his file for me and I learned that a sheriff's deputy picked him up on February 16, 2012, a year when nine out of every ten dogs at the shelter were euthanized, most within days or weeks of their arrival. It was a woman named Krista Lombardo, a Connecticut native who had relocated to Alexandria, who went to the shelter and saved Albie, and it was Krista who had made the short video that caused us to fall in love with him.

Krista, a Syracuse University graduate, first came to Alexandria to take a job as a television reporter, married, had children, and stayed. She considers herself a freelance rescuer and she regularly collaborates with Keri to get her dogs adopted, but she also sees herself as a volunteer at the shelter. She identified Albie as a dog she wanted to rescue — he was sweet tempered and "just wanted to be with you" — and pulled him shortly thereafter. Sometimes, in rescue lingo "pulled" literally means taken from the shelter to a foster home or another place where the dog will be safe from euthanasia. In Albie's case, it meant Krista came to the shelter and placed a "hold" on him. For two weeks, he was still eligible for local adoption. He wasn't adopted, so Krista began the process of adopting him herself with the intention of getting him into the Labs4rescue program. The adoption was formalized on March 26, 2012. Krista, who enjoys a good working relationship with shelter director Wimbley, persuaded him to allow Albie to remain at the shelter while she and Keri sought an adopter. Depending on space availability, Krista has been allowed to keep dogs there for up to a year.

Part of her agreement with Henry Wimbley was that she would buy Albie's food and take care of his medical needs. Two to three times a week, she came and took him for walks.

When I met with Krista in Dr. Haas's office, I asked her how she came up with the name Albie. It was, she told me, the name of one of the sons on the television program *The Real Housewives of New Jersey*. My wife, Judy, and I both grew up in New Jersey so it seemed fitting somehow.

"The shelter needs a rescue connection to look good," Sara says as we continue our tour. "As a shelter director, you want someone who does rescue work you can control and you can take credit for saving dogs. Mr. Wimbley and I use each other to mutual advantage," she says. "He gives me a lot of leeway and I try and be as respectful as I can be. As a physician, I'm used to being in control, so it's hard to let other people run the show, especially when you know there are things they could be doing to improve infection control." As with Krista, Henry Wimbley will hold dogs for Sara as long as he has the space, and she keeps the dogs moving to fosters or forever families.

One of the biggest challenges Sara and Keri face is that more than 80 percent of adult dogs (two years and up) at the Alexandria shelter are heartworm positive. Heartworm is not directly passed from dog to dog, as are parvo and distemper; it's transmitted when a mosquito bites an infected dog and then bites another dog.

Heartworm is treatable, but the treatment can be difficult for the dog. The disease can also be fatal.

"We treat those we pull from the shelter," Sara says, "but we avoid testing them in the shelter because once they test positive, they're euthanized because people generally won't adopt heartworm positive dogs. It costs us an average of two hundred dollars a dog to treat heartworm, and post treatment the dogs need to reduce activity and be kept calm for a long period. We then retest to be as sure as we can be that there's no active disease, and then the dog is ready for adoption.

"The problems here with respect to our dog and cat population are educational and financial," Sara continues. "When we moved here I was shocked at the high price of veterinary care. It was higher than where we were living in Tampa. There were no low cost spay and neuter clinics. And the average annual family income in this area is about $29,000. A lot of people are living on some sort of public assistance." It's no wonder taking care of animals isn't a high priority.

After we leave the shelter, we make a mad dash to the school where Sara's daughters,

Campbell and Sydney, are waiting to be picked up. They're very personable and talkative. They refer to me as "Mr. Peter."

The four of us drive to a private dog shelter called Boudreaux's Animal Rescue Krewe (BARK), also located in Alexandria.[21] Owned by the Long family, BARK is a private, nonprofit organization devoted to saving dogs from neglect and/or abuse and maintaining shelter for them until a loving home is found. BARK is a no-kill facility. Dogs here are generally adopted out in Canada and there's a large trailer used for transport parked outside.

Again, as we enter the kennel areas, the barking nearly drowns out our conversation. Though the dogs here are safe from euthanasia, and there are more obvious efforts at infection control, such as bleach baths for dipping shoes before moving from one section to another, there's only so much you can do to make a concrete kennel a place where you'd be happy to see a dog spend

21. A krewe typically refers to an organization that puts on a parade or ball during Carnival season; it's a term commonly associated with Mardi Gras in New Orleans. But it's also used loosely to mean team or group. Boudreaux was a boxer the Longs, who started the shelter, rescued years ago.

months or years. Some of the dogs here are aggressive pit bulls and cannot be adopted out; they will remain here indefinitely. One of the pit bulls, an absolutely sweet seven-year-old named Pearl, has scars where her muzzle was wired shut.

There are trade-offs to be made everywhere in rescue. Sara admires what the Longs are doing, but points out that when you are 100 percent committed to no-kill and you can't move the dogs along to homes, perhaps because the dog is aggressive, that's space that isn't available to another dog sitting in a high-kill shelter that might be highly adoptable.

"So," I ask Sara toward the end of a long day, "why animals?" There are many people, including children, in need right here in central Louisiana. Why devote all this time and effort to saving animals? It's the same question I put to Greg when I visited him in Zanesville.

"As a physician I deal with people all the time," she answers. "But these animals are a population of unconditionally loving creatures. When I see an animal abused, it's like child abuse or elder abuse. Animals are innocent and have no control over what happens to them. You can personally impact

170

many lives in the ER, but there's a lot of satisfaction in helping helpless creatures.

"When I die, I want to know I did something to change this little world," she adds. "When you connect a family and a dog and you hear from them afterward, there's a feeling of great satisfaction."

Natchitoches, in west-central Louisiana, is the oldest city in the state. Its small downtown on the banks of the Cane River, home to several historic plantations, is beautiful and charming.

I made the one-hour drive north from Alexandria to Natchitoches to meet a young man named Clarence Nash, who goes by CJ. When we met, CJ, then eighteen, had just started his freshman year at the University of Louisiana at Monroe.

Four months earlier, CJ's dog, a silver Lab mix named Mia, had given birth to ten puppies near his family's trailer home fifteen miles outside of town. Five of them were the S puppies — Sally, Sylvia, Sully, Seth, and Salyna — we took on board Greg's truck in Alexandria a few weeks before, most bound for the Rhode Island adoption event. I made the connection to CJ through Rae McManus of Colfax, who saw a picture of me with one of the puppies, Salyna, on

Greg's Rescue Road Trips Facebook page and got in touch with me.

For years Rae has been active in several rescue and animal welfare organizations — she's the vice president of the Coalition of Louisiana Animal Advocates and founder of the Heart of Louisiana Humane Society — and she messaged me to tell me she had had a hand in saving Mia's litter. I was curious to learn more, and she offered to put me in touch with CJ, a friend of her daughter's since grade school.

I doubted CJ would be willing to talk to me — a stranger and writer from up north — because he had little to gain from doing so. But I was wrong, and he so impressed me during our phone conversation, I was determined to meet him.

CJ is articulate and charming, and looks scholarly in his large eyeglasses. The trailer home where he grew up is one of three on the property where numerous relatives live. A few junked cars sit in the expansive yard where the puppies were born; CJ's father, Clarence Sr., works as a short-haul trucker. His mother, Joanna, is a supervisor for the Louisiana Department of Children and Family Services. He has two younger brothers, Devon, fifteen, and eight-year-old Bryant.

Mia's recent litter was her second in the last two years; the first comprised three puppies, one of which, Sasha, the Nashes kept. Like Salyna, she is yellowish white with a blue tongue. Mia and Sasha are what is known in the South as a "yard dogs."

"Where we live, this is how dogs live," says CJ. "People aren't interested in having house dogs. You don't worry about shedding and pooping. We love our dogs, but we don't see them living with us in the house. They're not part of the family the way your dogs are. The dogs take care of themselves. You'll do much more to care for a dog."

I ask him why they haven't spayed Mia since they obviously didn't want more puppies.

"To come up with $150 to spay Mia is a bit of trouble," says CJ. "We live on a check-to-check basis. And it's hard to get to the vet because my parents both work, I don't drive, and the vet's office is closed after work hours. But based on this experience with Mia and the puppies, I know we should spay her.

"I've had Mia since she was just three weeks old," he continues. "I talk to her like I talk to my brothers. It's personal, and she'll look back and listen as I talk; she reacts. She seems human to me in that way.

173

But most people here don't spend time like that with their dogs. They're just animals. Mia is free and she enjoys it, always running and playing. But it would be less worry if she were spayed.

"Some people around here keep all the puppies their dogs have and feed them what little they can until the puppies just run off," he adds. "Some try to breed them, but mostly they just leave the dogs to fend for themselves. Some are hauled off to the shelter or are just ditched in the woods or left by the side of the road. You can't treat another living being that way."

Though CJ spends a lot of time with the dogs, they aren't well socialized. Mia wouldn't let me approach her, and when I reached out to pet Sasha, with CJ and Bryant both holding her, she snarled.

After Mia's second litter was born in early March 2012, CJ's father told him to get rid of them by taking them to the local pound.

"I knew there was a better, more humane way than taking them to the shelter where they'd be killed immediately," he says. "I knew Ms. McManus could help or would know someone who could help, like Ms. Keri Toth." CJ emailed Rae and asked for help.

Rae drove out to the Nashes shortly

thereafter and noticed the puppies were mostly Lab. Over the years Keri, through Labs4rescue, has helped Rae place Labs she's rescued and they collaborate frequently. She called Keri, who provided vaccines and medication to deworm the puppies and Rae vaccinated and dewormed them at the Nashes herself.

"My dad wanted to know who was paying for all this," CJ says. "When he found out it was all paid for by Ms. Toth, he said to me, 'You really know how to deal with this don't you?' " The son had proved himself to his father. "I told my dad, I'll take care of it and you relax."

When the pups were about six weeks old, Rae brought three to Keri for fostering at Dr. Haas's clinic; the others remained at the Nashes until they were about nine weeks, when they joined their siblings in Alexandria — a friend of the Nashes also adopted one. Three weeks later, all had been spayed and neutered. Keri's daughter, Chelsea, adopted one and Seth had an adopter waiting for him in Massachusetts. We took five aboard Greg's truck in Alexandria on that rainy Wednesday morning. The other three joined Keri and Greta in the van for the drive to Rhode Island for the adoption event that Sunday. There was no doubt the puppies would be snatched up quickly, especially Salyna, the beautiful yellow one. And she was.

5
LONE STAR STATE OF MIND

Now that we've seen the world Keri and Sara operate in, and how many of their dogs get from the streets and shelters to Greg's truck, let's rewind and rejoin Greg during my trip with him several weeks earlier. At 10:30 a.m., three and half hours after we started boarding dogs in Alexandria, we pull out for Baytown, Texas, 225 miles away. Getting all of Keri's dogs on board and their paperwork sorted out has taken longer than expected. Greg tries hard to keep to his schedule because he always has people waiting on him up and down the line, and delays, especially avoidable ones, drive him up the wall.

Baytown is where Greg picks up dogs from Kathy Wetmore's Houston Shaggy Dog Rescue, and occasionally some dogs from Nutmeg Rescue, run by Tom English, a math professor at a community college in Texas City, about forty miles southeast of

Houston. Sometimes there are dogs from other area rescues too. After the pick-ups in Baytown, we'll drive two hundred miles back east to Lafayette, where we'll spend the night, just ninety miles south of where the day began in Alexandria.

Greg makes this 425-mile drive to Baytown and back to Louisiana whether it's to pick up one dog or twenty. It's on his schedule and he's committed to it, even if it costs a couple hundred dollars in diesel and the entire day to get there and back. He has to be in Lafayette by Wednesday night because Thursdays begin bright and early with pickups at Lafayette Animal Aid, a rescue organization located in Carencro, in Lafayette Parish, just north of the city of Lafayette.

As we hop on the interstate, Greg takes a phone call from Deb Cook Keavy, a Labs4rescue adoption coordinator who lives in Connecticut but arranges adoptions from south-central Louisiana. When he hangs up, Greg tells me we'll be picking up Sadie, a four-year-old female yellow Lab, tomorrow in Hammond, Louisiana, about an hour east of Baton Rouge. Sadie is a special case. She has epilepsy. Anxiety can trigger her seizures and transport can be stressful since it's a new and foreign environment where the only people around the dogs are strangers. Since we have an extra body (mine), Greg has assured Deb that Sadie will ride in the cab next to me on Tommy's mattress to ensure she has quiet and human companionship along the way. Plus, we can keep an eye on her in case she has a seizure. Greg informs me I'll also be responsible for administering her epilepsy medication twice a day.

Sadie's story is different from most but sad nonetheless. She had a family in Louisiana who raised her from puppyhood and

179

loved her. But the three-year-old son developed severe dog allergies, and they couldn't keep her. At the thought of Sadie being abruptly separated from the only family she's known, my compassion leaps for this dog I haven't even met yet. *What,* I wonder, *goes through a dog's mind at times like this?* Her new forever family, Brenda Byers-Britney and daughter, Elizabeth, of Middle Haddam, Connecticut, will be waiting for her at Rocky Hill.

While on the road, Greg regularly checks on the dogs. When we stop shortly after noon a few miles east of the Texas line, it's hot and humid, but the trailer is cool thanks to the four generator-powered air-conditioning units. In the trailer, I take Salyna out of her kennel. She appeared frightened when we boarded her a few hours ago and still seems on edge and unhappy. Sensing my concern, Greg suggests I have her ride with me in the cab. Greg can be hard to read sometimes, and at first I think he might be joking at what he sees as my undue concern. After all, he's seen tens of thousands of dogs on transport and not all of them are going to be happy campers all the time. Aware that perhaps he's just indulging me and trying to make *me* comfortable (never mind the dog), I take Salyna with me. Tommy takes over the driving, Greg is sitting on the mattress behind me and to my left, and I am in the passenger seat with Salyna on my lap.

Greg can occasionally show flashes of irritation, especially when he senses naïveté about dogs. Salyna trembled as I climbed up into the cab and tried to get her settled in my arms.

"She's so scared," I say.

"She's *not* scared," Greg snaps, "and I take offense, *I really do,* that you think one of my dogs is scared!"

It's true. What do I know? At this point in my life, I'd seen all of forty dogs loaded onto transport. Greg, meanwhile, has transported more than thirty thousand dogs over ten years and he doesn't confuse a dog's mild trepidation with fear.

Scared or not, Salyna had been upgraded to first class, riding in my lap, while the other Alexandria dogs ride in kennels in the trailer. The contact calms her and she sits quietly in my arms for the next couple of hours as we pass the massive oil refineries along Interstate 10 near Lake Charles, Louisiana, heading for Baytown. With each passing mile, I find myself growing more and more attached to Salyna and she seems to be enjoying the company too.

At 1:30 p.m., we cross into Texas and stop for fuel. It's been more than a thousand miles since our last fill up in Ohio and that means another receipt for over five hundred dollars. We check the dogs again, making sure each has water before driving the last half hour to the parking lot of a Cracker Barrel, the pickup point for all the Texas dogs that will be joining us. It's three o'clock.

Rescue involves *a lot* of physical work, especially hauling dogs here and there virtually all day, every day. So it's amazing that a widow in her early sixties, like Kathy Wetmore of Houston Shaggy Dog Rescue, does all the work herself. A native of the British Isle of Wight and a self-described "control freak," she is hands-on in every aspect of her rescue work: she walks through the shelters looking for dogs to rescue; manages the adoption process and the website, for which she does all the photography; shepherds her dogs to their veterinary appointments; and personally brings the dogs heading north to meet Greg every other Wednesday.

"I can't afford a screwup when I'm shipping *dogs*," she says.

She's a tall, broad-shouldered woman, and doesn't move easily. Her gait is slightly labored, and the heat and humidity in Houston much of the year make the physical part of her job all the harder. But that doesn't stop her. In 2013, she adopted out about 210 dogs to various parts of the United States; all those bound for the Northeast traveled with Greg.

Kathy has fewer dogs than usual traveling with Greg this week: about a half-dozen including shy Carina, a griffon/sheepdog mix; Maggie May, a poodle mix; and Willis, a shaggy, white bichon mix with cataracts, a dog Kathy described to me on the phone a couple of weeks earlier as "the happiest little guy."

Willis wasn't one of Houston's staggering 1.2 million strays. His owner surrendered him to the large shelter known as BARC (Bureau of Animal Regulation and Control) where strays picked up by the city's animal control officers are also brought. Kathy visits BARC regularly and pulls most of the dogs she rescues from there.

"I was walking through the holding kennels," she told me on the phone, "and I saw this happy dog. His skin was terrible and he was missing fur on the back. But he was just as happy as could be. The shelter adoption coordinator told me, 'His time is up today,' and I took him."

That Willis's time was up was no surprise to Kathy. He was about eight, and older dogs, or "senior dogs" as they are called, are harder to place because their life expectancy is relatively short. But there are adopters who are keen to give them a chance to enjoy their last few years. And that's exactly who Kathy was hoping to find for Willis.

But first she had to clean him up. Willis was in bad shape. As soon as she pulled Willis from BARC, he began treatment for a bad case of flea dermatitis, and Kathy brought him to a veterinary ophthalmologist to see if his cataracts could be treated as well. Surgery was ruled out; Willis's eyes didn't drain well enough, but medications have helped. His vision is passable, but he's nearly blind in one eye.

Kathy makes investments like this all the time to get her dogs ready for adoption. She's a successful real estate agent, once the top-grossing broker in the state. In an average year, she spends $200,000 from her own pocket on veterinary care. She's spent as much as $4,000 on a single dog's dental work. She has about a half-dozen veterinarians in the city she uses, including specialists, and all discount their services. Kathy is yet another example of the many selfless people who work in the rescue world.

Before joining Greg on the road, I also spoke to both Willis's adopting family, Mary Ellen and Phil Gambutti, of Easton, Pennsylvania, and the young woman, Tilani Pomirko, who had been fostering Willis for almost a year while Kathy was attending to his medical needs and reviewing applications from potential adopters who had seen Willis's profile on her website.

Tilani is a vet tech for one of the veterinarians Kathy uses, and she fosters special-needs dogs for Kathy, those with behavioral issues who need more socialization before being adopted, amputees, and, in Willis's case, some who need ongoing medical treatment.

"I hadn't met Willis when I agreed to foster him," Tilani told me. "But Kathy said he was the happiest dog she'd ever met. And he *is* the happiest little dog. When he first came to the clinic, he played with Nugget, a cat we had there. We always want to see how a dog does with cats before adopting them out, and he prefers cats to dogs."

Tilani had no other pets during the year she fostered Willis and she was dreading saying good-bye to him. Her voice quavered and she sobbed gently through much of our conversation.

"The paperwork said 'owner surrender due to behavioral issues,' but I never observed any problems," Tilani told me. It's not uncommon for owners, perhaps embarrassed by their decision to surrender a dog they don't want, perhaps for financial reasons, perhaps for no reason other than their own convenience, to fib to shelter personnel.

"When Willis is gone, my apartment will be empty," she said. "I wanted to adopt him, but I work twelve hours a day and Willis spends those hours with a dog buddy in a kennel and in the yard. Then I come home tired. It's not fair to him. He needs someone who will love him unconditionally, which I do, but also someone who can dote on him, which I can't." Tilani's selflessness is deeply touching; she so clearly adores Willis but is honest enough with herself to know he could have a better life elsewhere.

"I've been thinking about what the transition will be like for Willis," she added. "But he's very adaptable to change and to new people. I'm so excited for him going on this journey. He always goes with the flow. It'll be harder on me than on him. But I want to tell him it will be okay." Tilani was strug-

186

gling through her tears at this point. "I want to tell him, 'It will be a long trip, but you'll be in a good home.' You wish you could make them understand: 'It'll be a long and scary trip, but you're going to have the best life.' "

When we arrive in Baytown, Kathy and Tilani are there with Willis, the other dogs leaving today, and Willis's lamb chop toy, his favorite. Willis is exactly as advertised: despite all the commotion, the big truck half-filled with barking dogs, and the new people, he's a happy little warrior who seems to enjoy every minute. As I would learn over the next three days on transport, that mood almost never changes. Invariably, some of the dogs are quiet and withdrawn, some rambunctious and some just calm, but every time I passed Willis's kennel during the trip, he would show his excitement by marching in place, like a little drummer boy. He should have been wearing a name tag with a happy face that said, "Hello, my name is Willis! What's yours?" because he seemed like he wanted to befriend everyone he met. There was no question Willis would be worthy of his new family, and given how thorough Kathy is, I was sure the Gambuttis would be worthy of him.

Willis was by all accounts such a special little guy that I wanted to know how the Gambuttis found him and why they wanted to adopt him, so I called them to learn more. Phil Gambutti is semiretired; Mary Ellen still has right-side paralysis from a stroke she suffered six years ago, which forced her to give up her work as a professional gardener and garden designer. The Gambuttis have had several dogs and cats over the years, including some who came to them with multiple health problems.

"We're very comfortable with dogs and have a lot of experience with dogs with special needs," Mary Ellen told me when we spoke. "It's been about a year since our two cats died a short time apart, and I miss having a companion animal."

On the recommendation of a friend, the Gambuttis went to Kathy's website. Because of Mary Ellen's disability, the Gambuttis needed a small dog, one Mary Ellen could handle. A number of people in the fifty-five and over community where they live have bichons. "Willis just spoke to us," said Mary Ellen. "He was just so cute."

Kathy spoke to the Gambuttis' veterinarian and their references, including some who had previously been Houston Shaggy Dog Rescue adopters. After Kathy approved their application, the Gambuttis and Tilani spoke often by phone and exchanged emails.

"She's done a super job prepping me," Mary Ellen said. "About his needs, his meds, his personality. For example, we know he loves cream cheese, so she told us to give him his prednisone [a steroid he takes for his cataracts] with some cream cheese."

As it is for most adopters, the wait can be excruciating. Mary Ellen and Phil could hardly wait for the day when Greg's truck rolled into Allentown, Pennsylvania, with Willis. And Willis? He seemed excited from the moment I met him in Baytown. He was doing his little marching in place and almost seemed to be saying, "I like that truck! Let's go!"

By about 4:00 p.m., eleven of the twelve dogs boarding in Baytown are settled into their kennels in the trailer. But there's one dog with the wrong paperwork. He comes from a rescue organization that's using Greg for the first time. We wait for the next forty minutes while the woman who brought the dog to the truck tries to get someone — it appears to be her boyfriend from hearing her half of the conversation — to take pictures of the correct paperwork with his iPhone and email the images to Greg. He's supposed to have the hard copies, but Greg agrees to take the dog if he has electronic copies with hard copies to follow.

During the wait, I cuddle with Salyna, who seems noticeably less nervous than she was a few hours ago. I take her for a walk around the parking lot as several passersby stop to admire the beautiful little puppy, and I chat with Tom English. Tom isn't sending any dogs north with Greg this time, but he's come so we can meet face-to-face. I'm planning to come back in a few weeks and spend several days with him and Kathy Wetmore and observe their work up close.

Our wait is to no avail. Eventually, Greg decides we can't delay any longer; they'll have to send the dog with the missing paperwork on the next trip. The rescue volunteer who brought him understands, but there's something sad about seeing a dog so close to starting his journey home get back in the car he came in. But Greg's doing the right thing. He just can't risk taking him without the legally required documentation. If we didn't have such a full load, Greg might be more aggravated than he is because he doesn't charge if the dog doesn't ride. It does, however, mean we'll get into Lafayette an hour later than planned, which means one less hour of sleep before waking at the break of dawn to pick up dogs there.

It's a little past five o'clock and we're back on Interstate 10 for the four-hour drive to Lafayette, and Salyna, even calmer now, is back in the trailer in one of the kennels. Surveying the cab, I see an extraordinary assortment of food for us has appeared, seemingly out of nowhere. Boxes and bags from Whole Foods bulge with goodies quite unlike the usual trucker's fare: artichoke, feta, and lemon fritters; fresh fruit; an assortment of cookies and muffins; and crab cakes, among other items. Greg grins when he sees me eyeing this impromptu buffet and tells me Kathy loads them up every trip. She fills a large cooler with food, Greg drops it off empty the next trip, and she delivers another. It's more than a cut above what we've been eating the past two days. Kathy's generosity toward Greg — remember, she rescued him from bankruptcy by keeping him on the road when his truck needed a $7,000 repair — is deeply appreciated. Greg would drive to the end of the earth for Kathy and her dogs.

By the time we get back in the cab in Baytown, Greg, Tommy, and I have worked up a good sweat. The weather is hot, in the mid-eighties, though not as hot as it's going to be as the southern summer gets into high gear.

"If it's really hot, I may check the dogs every half hour," Greg tells me as we rumble down the interstate. "It can be over a hundred degrees with 100 percent humidity outside, and I'll be running all the generators to max out the AC." The hot weather is harder on Greg and Tommy than the dogs. These are southern dogs, used to living in the heat, and the trailer stays nice and cool. But getting dozens of dogs on and off the truck for a walk is *a lot* of physical labor for two men, especially in brutal heat.

About halfway to Lafayette, in the Cajun country of southwestern Louisiana, we stop at a service station with a large, grassy field nearby. We have about fifty dogs on board and it's time for each to get a short walk. There's no fixed time interval for walks; it depends on many factors: weather, traffic, and time of day. If he were stopping every few hours to walk eighty dogs, the trip north might take eight days or even more. Instead, the goal is to make the trip as short as possible to minimize the time the dogs spend in the kennels while making sure they get occasional breaks. Throughout the journey, the dogs get snacks and water, and their kennels are cleaned as needed.

It's still hot and humid, even in the early evening, but Greg and I each take the dogs, one at a time, for a walk while Tommy changes paper in the kennels and makes sure each has water. At some stops like this, curious passersby will come over to find out what's going on, but not this time. We're in a pretty isolated spot away from the gas pumps.

As we do the walks, I'm once again reminded of how physical this work is, lifting dogs out of kennels, securing the leashes and sometimes being towed along by a large dog very happy to be free of its kennel, so he or she can poop and pee freely.

Some dogs bound down the stairs of the truck; some have to be handed down into Greg's or my waiting arms. One dog, Zack, a cur, seems petrified as he climbs into my arms when Tommy hands him down to me. Jenna, a black Lab, just rolls over, wanting a belly rub. It's impossible not to get peed on or to get poop smeared on your shirt and shorts when you're handling so many dogs that have spent hours in kennels. Mix in the sweat from walking dozens of dogs in the

Louisiana heat with no shower for two days (and none to come for another two), and you have a recipe for an undeniably pungent yet oddly sweet smell. And yet, just as I am wondering how I'm going to go another two days without a shower, Greg ambles by with one of the dogs and says in all seriousness, "I pity people with real jobs."

Usually, of course, it's just Greg and Tommy getting all this done until they reach Birmingham, where the Angels arrive to help.

Once every dog has been walked and every kennel tended to, a process that takes about an hour and a half, we're back on the road. So far, except for the slight delays, everything is going smoothly.

But by the time we pull into Lafayette around 10:00 p.m., the hour's delay in Baytown has repercussions. A heavy downpour has caused the truck stop parking lot where Greg usually spends the night to be inundated. Since space is first-come, first-served, the few usable spaces are already taken. We have to double back toward Texas on Interstate 10 again; the nearest alternative is behind us and there's no guarantee there will be space there either. Greg's frustrated. Every hour of sleep matters, especially at this point because once we leave Lafayette tomorrow morning, the goal is for Greg and Tommy to switch off and drive straight through to Allentown, save for a couple of hours in Birmingham, where the Angels will help walk the dogs, a truck stop shower in southwestern Virginia, and the usual fuel, food, and bathroom stops, for both dogs and humans. If Greg and Tommy can't both grab enough sleep tonight, it could mean both are too tired to allow them to drive through the night tomorrow, even if they catnap during the day. They'll get to Gotcha Day by hook or by crook because the families are depending on them, but it could mean an even harder push for both men.

After backtracking about ten miles down Interstate 10 we finally find a spot. Greg and I head to the trailer as Tommy climbs into his berth in the cab. As usual, our appearance in the trailer sets off a ruckus among the dogs. Once again, it doesn't faze Greg a bit. Within thirty seconds of his head hitting the pillow, he is sound asleep, while I'm still unpacking my sleeping bag and doing my best with paper towels and a spray cleaner to make the floor where I'm going to sleep marginally acceptable given my high standards for cleanliness. It's been a long day since we boarded the first dogs in Alexandria and though I haven't been the one doing the driving, I could use some sleep.

Three hours later I'm still staring at the ceiling. It only took about half an hour after Greg fell asleep for all the dogs to settle down — all, that is, except one. With my legs wrapped like a mummy's in my sleeping bag and extended into the narrow space between the kennels, my nose about six inches from the snoozing yellow Lab named Tennessee, I listen as one little dog barks a high pitched yap hour after hour.

The dog doesn't sound particularly distressed, just eager for someone to play with. This is our first night with dogs in the trailer and I'm completely unsure what to do. If I weren't here, Greg would be sleeping regardless and the night would pass with or without the continued barking. But I desperately want to fall asleep, and unlike Greg, I can't sleep through the noise. Yet if I move to try and calm him, or her, I may rouse some of the other dogs, and they in turn could rouse still more, and then all hell might break out and, God forbid, wake Greg from a precious sleep. Even if I tiptoe over to the kennel, managing not to disturb any other dogs, unstrap the kennel from the wall, and bring him near me, will he calm down or just be barking even closer to my ear? And if I do, will Greg wake in the morning and be angry that I took it upon myself to move the kennel?

I finally decide the noisy status quo is intolerable and move as stealthily as possible to the kennel where the ruckus is coming from. It sounds like the bark of a small dog, which means he or she is likely on the top row where the smaller kennels sit. I manage not to disturb the other dogs, except for a whimper or two. And then I find the culprit who's keeping me awake. It's Willis, Mr. Happy himself! I open the kennel door to pet him, and he goes into his little-drummer-boy happy dance but surprisingly makes no effort, as many will when you open their kennel doors, to push his way out. When I think I have him settled, I close the kennel door and move as quietly as I can back toward my sleeping bag. Then, as soon as I slither back into the bag, he starts up again. Willis and I do this little *pas de deux* three or four times before I lift him from his kennel and hold him in the crook of my left arm. With my right, I reach into his kennel and realize the newspaper is wet, probably from spilling his water during his excited little dance but perhaps from more natural causes. With Willis still under my left arm, I gather up the newspapers and quietly walk to the back of the trailer, where there's a trash can and fresh newspaper. After re-papering his kennel, I put him back in and he settles down nicely at last.

For a couple of hours, all is quiet on the western front and I doze lightly and dream of clean sheets and fluffy pillows. Then, without warning, T-Bone, the fifty-pound fox hound–pointer mix, goes on a barking jag three feet from my head. *How,* I wonder, *does Greg sleep through all this?*

I know in part he's used to it and partly it's the sheer exhaustion of the work. I also know, from the time I rode with Greg for the *Parade* piece, that there are times in the trailer when it's eerily quiet — every dog asleep — and the only sound the hum of the generators.

But right now T-Bone is holding nothing back. I make my way over to his kennel on my knees and, with my fingers stretched through the kennel door, scratch him under his chin, which immediately calms him. But every time I withdraw and try to get back to my sleeping bag — which is not aptly named for a night like tonight — he starts howling again. Remarkably, even the dog in the next kennel, a yellow Lab named Baby Bella, sleeps soundly. But T-Bone just wants more, and for the next two hours, until about five thirty, I stroke his face and neck until he falls asleep at last. Unfortunately for me, we need to leave the truck stop in an hour so we can arrive at Lafayette Animal Aid where people and dogs are waiting on us. Fortunately for everyone, I'm not driving.

6
HOUSTON, YOU HAVE A PROBLEM

When I see Tadpole for the first time, he's sitting on a white plastic lawn chair on the front stoop of a one-story brick house in Houston's impoverished Fifth Ward. A tiny dachshund mix puppy about eight weeks old, Tadpole looks like a large but very cute rat because mange has denuded most of his body. A few stray hairs stick out from his head behind oversized ears. He's completely docile and doesn't move, except for a slight turn of his head as two strangers approach.

It's been several weeks since my trip with Greg from Ohio to New England ended (a trip we'll rejoin in Chapter 9), and I've returned to Texas, as I had to Louisiana, to learn more about Kathy Wetmore, Tom English, and others here who rescue the dogs who ride to their forever homes on Greg's truck from Baytown. I was especially eager to spend time in urban Houston and its surroundings and see its staggering dog

overpopulation problem for myself; I had been under the misimpression when I first started learning about rescue that it was primarily a rural problem. Houston proves that's not the case.

Kelle Davis and Alicia McCarty are part of small grassroots group of volunteers that comprise Forgotten Dogs of the Fifth Ward Project, a so-called "street" street rescue devoted to improving the lives of the stray and neglected dogs in one of Houston's most destitute and dangerous neighborhoods. The Fifth Ward is ground zero for Houston's 1.2 million strays that roam rubbish-strewn streets riddled with drugs and violent crime.

For the next few hours, I'll be riding along

with Kelle and Alicia in Alicia's SUV as they take to the streets of the Fifth Ward. Two teams from the Project patrol different parts of the neighborhood twice a week.

There are strays everywhere. When Kathy Wetmore of Houston Shaggy Dog Rescue brings me to meet Kelle and Alicia at the CVS just off the freeway, a thin, mangy female pit bull, nipples elongated from nursing a new litter, ears infested with mites, wanders the parking lot, licking at food scraps, while people come and go as if it were a perfectly ordinary sight. In the Fifth Ward, it is.

When Kelle and Alicia arrive they immediately pull a bag of dry food from the back of the car and spread some on the walkway just outside the drugstore entrance. The mama pit bull is calm but wary, and when she's had her fill, she walks off toward a busy four-lane road. We hold our breath as she trots right into the roadway, cars speeding by or slowing suddenly to avoid her, and then ambles off into a field across the way.

Kelle and Alicia know these streets and they know many of the dogs, for they have seen them before. Dog by dog, person by person, street by street, they are trying to make life just a little better. They drop off free dog food for people who can't afford it. Once they earn their trust, they'll urge spaying and neutering and offer information about how to get it done free or at very low cost. For those dogs living on the streets, they spread enough food on corners to last a couple of days. For those they can approach, they may administer vaccines to help stave off infectious disease or give oral medications to treat fleas or mange. One tiny step at a time, they are trying to educate people and alleviate misery for the dogs.

It was another dog we saw, also a dachshund mix, that led us to Tadpole. We spotted him running on the median strip of a busy road by the railroad tracks. Alicia had pulled the car over, concerned the dog was about to become roadkill. As she tried to coax the dog to her, a man wandered by and told us the dog lived just down the street. As it took off, we followed in the car until it entered the yard where Tadpole was sitting quietly in the white plastic chair. Alicia approached the house and rang the bell several times. No one answered. Kelle, a licensed vocational nurse, and Alicia, a nursing student, conferred. Tadpole wasn't long for this world. He was undernourished and his advanced mange reflected complete neglect. And there was no way of knowing if Tadpole belonged to the people in this house, or had just wandered there. Left untreated, the mange would likely lead to a slow, painful death from a secondary infection.

In the car, Tadpole takes a little bit of food — a good sign. He'll need to be isolated from other dogs at first in case he has parvo or distemper. Within minutes, Alicia, using her iPhone, has posted his picture on Facebook looking for a foster willing to take him in. But when we meet Kathy Wetmore for a late dinner that evening, she agrees, even though he isn't and won't be a shaggy dog, to make Tadpole one of her Houston Shaggy Dog rescues. He'll be in her care until he's healthy enough for adoption and the trip north with Greg.

Forgotten Dogs of the Fifth Ward Project doesn't pull dogs from shelters for adoption as traditional rescue organizations do; their focus is on doing what they can for the dogs on the street, but sometimes they remove those in especially dire straits, like Tadpole, in the hopes of nurturing them back to health and finding them a forever home, or getting them into the hands of another rescue organization, such as Houston

Shaggy Dog, that can assume that responsibility.

"If we see a dog in critical condition that won't make it unless we take it, we take the dog and fly by the seat of our pants, hoping to find a rescue that will take the dog and prepare it for adoption," Kelle explains. "And we use social media and our personal networks to try and find a foster or permanent home." In the past two years, the project has taken 520 dogs off the streets to save their lives.

"Seventy-five percent of the dogs we take in have broken limbs from being hit by cars or have BBs in them because they rummage through trash and people shoot at them," Kelle adds. "We work with seven different vets and they give us discounts. A single dog may cost us thousands of dollars. But we've been lucky; whenever we've needed money, someone has come forward to help."

"We have great supporters," Alicia states. "So many rescue organizations are behind on their vet bills. We don't have that problem. And we always find fosters. Boarding can be a huge expense for rescues."

Kelle founded the Project in 2006. She didn't set out to start a street rescue, but volunteered after Hurricane Katrina to help save animals displaced by the storm. While in New Orleans, she learned how to trap dogs that needed care or were being sought by their owners. Then she started getting calls from various rescue groups to help with trapping strays, and one of her assignments took her into the Fifth Ward, where she was astonished to see how many strays wandered the streets.

"It just evolved," she says by way of explaining how she ended up staying here to tackle this immense challenge. Like most rescue organizations, the Project tries to bite off a small piece of what they know is a much larger problem.

"Spay[ing and] neuter[ing] and education are the only solutions to this problem," Alicia says, "but we don't have the time or resources for that. We're just trying to help the dogs we see and we just see the tip of the iceberg. For every dog we see, there are ten more just like it. People here don't seem to notice the suffering of the dogs because their own lives are so hard."

Shortly after leaving CVS and the mama pit bull, we pull into the parking lot of an abandoned strip mall. Under the marquee of a defunct movie theater are two older homeless women lying on filthy mattresses. They appear to be in their sixties or seventies, but given their living conditions, it's hard to tell; they may have aged prematurely. A shopping cart filled with clothes and other belongings sits nearby, as do two dogs and three kittens. At our approach, the women sit up. Kelle and Alicia have spoken with them before and the relationship is cordial. Every week they bring food for the women's dogs, Sugar and Lucky, and they've persuaded the women to let them try and find someone who can take better care of the kittens. The women keep Sugar and the ironically named Lucky tied up close to them because kids on bikes ride by and try to hurt the dogs if they're near the street.

Seeing dogs living in squalor is hard enough; seeing these well-meaning, destitute women living in the same squalor is deeply disturbing. They seem to be trying their best to care for the animals, but they can't even take care of themselves. They are appreciative of Kelle and Alicia's help, and are receptive to their efforts.

"We feed as we see," Alicia explains when we're back in the car. "We're always finding new situations and new regulars."

A little farther away, we round a corner where Alicia mentions she saw a man running from an assailant firing shots last week.

Drug dealing is pervasive in the Fifth Ward — so is violence. There's a small pack of dogs Kelle and Alicia have been watching here, and sure enough they appear almost immediately. Alicia spreads some dog food on the ground and they circle us tentatively. Kelle has been trying to inoculate them to treat their mange, but they have to be calm and ready to be approached. Kelle and Alicia are still trying to earn their trust. Mange is relatively easy to treat but requires multiple treatments, so they'll hopefully be able to treat these same dogs again over the next few weeks.

As the dogs eat, I look around. These may be the forgotten dogs of Houston's Fifth Ward we're feeding, but all around are the forgotten people of America, mostly black and Hispanic, people living in dilapidated houses amid trash that has accumulated on nearly every street and in every ditch: old tires, chunks of concrete, rusting metal, building materials, mattresses, broken glass, plastic, almost every kind of detritus imaginable. I also notice dogs everywhere — lurking behind trees, asleep under cars, chained up in yards, in playgrounds, parks, and even in the openings of abandoned houses. Freight trains rumble through the neighborhood on tracks just twenty feet from the nearest houses, whistles blaring and shaking the ground. The poverty here is a grinding, grim, hopeless one, sadly just a few miles from the corporate headquarters of the world's richest energy companies and the opulent homes of their executives. It's a Third World ward in a First World city. For Alicia it still doesn't justify the neglect and abuse of dogs she sees in the Fifth Ward every week.

"I try not to be a judgmental asshole," she says as we resume our patrol, referring to how dogs are treated here, "but it's hard. I'm pretty jaded about people at this point."

"This is a people problem, not a BARC problem," she adds, referring to Houston's major shelter, which sits at the edge of the Fifth Ward. "We can't adopt our way out of this. It's too big."

Our next stop is a short street abutting the railroad tracks. A long freight train slowly rumbles its way through the neighborhood. Here we find Kaiser, a thirteen-year-old, unaltered male hound mix with advanced heartworm disease, pulmonary hypertension (caused by heartworms), a badly infected broken tooth, and a tumor in his mouth that has given him a snaggle-tooth.

Though heartworm is, as noted, easily

prevented with a monthly, chewable tablet, it is endemic in the South. Heartworm is also treatable in the earlier stages, but once advanced, the worms clog the heart and can infiltrate the lungs.

Kaiser isn't a stray; his owner has lived on this street all his life, as has Kaiser. Kelle and Alicia have been bringing food for him for several weeks. Alicia is visibly upset and it's easy to see why; Kaiser lumbers and his breathing is labored. It's horrible to see such a sweet creature in such pain.

"He's dying," she says, her voice filled with a mix of anger and frustration, "and he'll die right here on the street. I just want to bring him home. I want him to know a little bit of love, a full belly, and a soft bed before he goes."

Looking at Kaiser, it occurs to me it's probably been fifty years since I've seen an unaltered adult male dog, yet I've already seen dozens this evening. When we were kids growing up in New Jersey in the 1950s and 1960s we used to giggle when we'd see a dog with its testicles bouncing around as he ran. That's when it hits me how different the spay/neuter issue plays out in the South versus the North. You can spend decades in the Northeast and never see a stray, let alone an unneutered male dog.

■ ■ ■

As early evening approaches and the heat subsides a bit, more and more dogs emerge from the shadows. It's eerie; they just seem to materialize from everywhere and nowhere. Almost all show signs of mange, fleas, and other biting insects; many have scratched themselves raw.

A little farther down the road, we spot a dog about to dart between the wheels of a moving train and a young boy of about eight or nine trying to scare it away from the tracks, a small act of humanity on what has been an evening filled with inhumanity. When the dog is safely out of harm's way, Alicia pulls the car over and yells, "Thank you." The boy waves in response and disappears.

Kelle and Alicia now look for a very pregnant boxer they've seen regularly at the same intersection. On foot, they're trying to find her when a woman emerges from her house on the corner and tells them the dog delivered her puppies a couple of days ago under an abandoned house across the street. Houses don't have basements here and most sit a few feet off the ground. If there's an opening, dogs can find shelter from the elements underneath. There are several places where the wood cladding has rotted or been torn away, and Kelle and Alicia are peering inside with flashlights for signs of the mama and her litter. After a few minutes, Alicia spots her and coaxes her slowly toward an opening in the wood planks. She sticks her head out and looks around. She doesn't appear aggressive so much as exhausted, but she's going to be protective of her puppies so the approach has to be as gentle as possible. Her mate soon joins her. Both heads show signs of mites and other insect bites. Slowly Kelle and Alicia lure them out with food, so they can better assess the dogs' conditions. They're frustrated a boxer rescue refused to take these two for adoption because without docked tails they weren't "boxer enough."

Once they've been drawn out from under the house, Kelle and Alicia get a better look. The mama's teats are enormous; she may have mastitis. The papa has severe mange, which is keeping him from gaining weight and he appears weak and thin. His skin is covered with small sores. Like the people around them, these dogs have been living a tough life.

As the dogs eat, Kelle sits on the curb, drawing deeply on a cigarette. Sometimes the work is so draining, so overwhelming, a person just needs to sit down and pause.

Microscopic lice transmit mange, and the papa needs to be treated or the pups will become infected. But he's very skittish and moves away whenever Kelle approaches. They decide to try and get a slip leash around his neck when he returns to the food. Dogs living like this can be unpredictable, but these are two gutsy, fearless women. In fact, I feel safer on these streets in their company than I would alone — key to their continued presence here is that they aren't timid and they move around like they belong here, projecting an aura both non-threatening and assertive at the same time.

When the papa returns to the food, Kelle gently dangles the slip leash in front of him and passes the loop over his head and under his neck and secures it. He resists a little at first, but remains calm as Kelle deftly gives him a shot of ivermectin, an antiparasitic. Kelle knows the ivermectin could be fatal if the dog has heartworms, which is very likely, but it's a calculated risk. Better, she says, a quick death from the ivermectin than a slow, painful death from heartworms. She also uses her fingers to expose the gums of the mama; they're pale from anemia. When they first saw this dog, she also had the beginnings of an embedded collar. Many young dogs are forsaken still wearing collars, and as they grow, the skin gradually grows around the collar. Usually surgery is required to remove it. In this case, people who Kelle and Alicia had been leaving dog food for, and who were able to approach the dog, removed the collar and treated the wound with peroxide and antibiotic ointment.

"We picked up one dog with a chain completely embedded in its neck," says Alicia. "Her face was so swollen she looked like her head was going to explode."

Any sign a dog is being properly cared for draws praise from Kelle and Alicia, a man walking a dog on a leash or a dog with a current rabies tag on its collar, for example. These small signs of responsibility are so rare here they stand out.

Down yet another street, we see a large dog that has a smaller one pinned to the ground in the culvert that stretches in front of the yards. From the car Alicia tries to startle it so the smaller dog will be released. Scanning the street, I see at last a dozen strays wandering about in every direction. A young boy of about ten wanders into the yard.

"Are these your dogs?" Alicia asks. "One

of them was beating up the other."

Sheepishly he says yes, they are his dogs.

"We're going to give them some food, okay?"

We hop out of the car. Tadpole is now asleep on the floor, wrapped in a towel. As Alicia spreads some food on the ground, Kelle scans the street, making a quick assessment of the curious dogs slowly walking in our direction. The first to the food is a muscular pit bull whose body language concerns Kelle. She tells us to keep our distance. There's no argument.

As we head back to the car, the young boy's mother emerges from the house.

"You need to get these dogs spayed and neutered," Kelle tells her. "We can help you with that. We'll come back." She thanks us for the food and we're off.

It's nearly 8:00 p.m., and we're supposed to meet Kathy Wetmore and Tom English for dinner in a few minutes but we're running late. As we head for the freeway, we see an older man in a ball cap, shorts, compression stockings, and flip-flops walking with an unleashed pit bull in a small field near the freeway entrance. Unable to tear herself away, Alicia pulls over, rolls down her window and asks the man if he needs food for the dog.

"Oh, yes, ma'am," he says. "I can really use some help with this dog. I have some burn injuries and this dog was abused and abandoned, and they put me in that roach-infested house over there and they say I can't keep a dog there."

It's not clear who "they" are, but the man is polite and articulate. He's missing most of his teeth, save for a few on the lower left side of his jaw. He says the dog's name in Sasha.

"These people over there had him for fighting," he says, pointing at the dog's ears, which have been crudely docked with a sharp instrument. Fighting dogs often have their ears clipped to keep opponents from latching onto them. "But he wouldn't fight so they abandoned him and I'm trying to take care of him."

As we talk, the dog, which wandered over with an old empty beer can in its mouth, is scratching furiously.

"That dog has fleas and mange," Kelle explains after she's gotten out of the car to have a closer look. The man is listening intently. He clearly wants to help this dog.

"If it's okay with you, I'm going to give him some medicine for the fleas that will work almost immediately. And I'll give him an injection that will help with the mange."

"Oh, that would be wonderful, ma'am, thank you, thank you," he replies. "I knew there was a reason I got up this afternoon." Kelle gives him a bag of dog food and a plastic syringe with an oral medication to help with the mange.

"Now, give him this in two weeks. Squirt it into the corner of his mouth, OK?"

"Yes, ma'am. Thank you, thank you. I know it's a little late but happy Fourth of July!"

Now we are officially late for dinner with Kathy and Tom and the restaurant is fifteen minutes away. But we're not done yet. Just as we approach the freeway on-ramp, Alicia suddenly veers sharply to the right.

"Oh my God, oh my God," she shrieks. "There's a dog on the ramp! He's going to get run over! Oh no, no, no!"

She does a quick circle around, stops the car by a vacant lot across the way, jumps out, and begins crossing a wide street toward the entrance to the on-ramp. There, huddled against a concrete embankment supporting the freeway, is a medium-sized black dog lying on a narrow berm, just inches off the ramp.

This is a dangerous situation for the dog and for Alicia. If she spooks the dog, it may run right into traffic, but approaching slowly means Alicia is vulnerable to high-speed traffic entering the freeway. Kelle tries to keep her from crossing, but she's already halfway there. The dog doesn't bolt, but Alicia is now crouched next to the dog at the edge of the ramp. I see a panel truck approaching and step into the road and wave my arms to slow it down.

The dog is wearing a collar, and Alicia leads it back to the vacant lot near the car. She puts some food out. The dog is very thin and has large scars on its head and bald spots covered with scabs.

I'm puzzled when Kelle removes the collar, the only way we might restrain the dog if it decides to head back into harm's way.

"It's just something I do," she says. "This dog used to belong to someone, but they gave up on it." My sense is that removing the collar is Kelle's way of setting the dog free from a past life in which it was never valued. After eating, the dog walks slowly back into the neighborhood and away from the freeway.

When she sees my confused look, she says, "I can't take him. I already have forty at home that need homes. This is the hard part; we have nowhere to take him." It's one thing to hear statistics (like the 1.2 million strays on Houston's streets), but ironically, the magnitude of the tragedy can only be appreciated when you look at the small picture. It's much easier to wrap your head, and your heart, around the suffering of one desperate animal than to try and fathom a million or more.

"It haunts you," Alicia says to me. "No matter how much you do, it's never enough and you feel like a piece of shit."

And with that, Kelle, Alicia, Tadpole, and I head off, quite late, for dinner with Kathy Wetmore and Tom English.

After an eye-opening and depressing day, dinner brings some happier news, a welcome relief, especially for Kelle and Alicia: Kathy offers to take Tadpole (a name she bestowed on him right after seeing him), nurse him back to health, and find a home for him through Houston Shaggy Dog Rescue. If all goes well, in a couple of months Tadpole will be on his way north with Greg.

The next morning, Kathy and I bring Tadpole and Bonnie and Lonnie, two puppies with scabies — "scabies babies" she calls them — a contagious skin ailment spread by mites, to the vet. Kathy gives the vet carte blanche with Tadpole; she wants a

219

thorough exam, the appropriate vaccines, and to begin treatment of his mange and whatever other ailments they may find. Then we drive a half hour to north Houston to yet another vet to pick up three puppies that have been spayed and neutered and who will be traveling with Greg next week to foster homes in Connecticut. Kathy uses this vet for most of the spaying and neutering because he's less expensive than some of the other vets closer to downtown where she lives.

By 11:00 a.m., we've been to three different veterinarian's offices. Few people adopting dogs up north realize how much has been invested by rescue organizations to save their dog and ensure its health. Adoption fees tend to be in the $400–500 range, but the medical bills are often far higher.

Like Keri Toth in Louisiana, Kathy's life seems to be one long, endless errand. She's constantly picking up and dropping off dogs at vets, day cares, foster homes, and with Greg in Baytown. At any given time, Kathy has dozens of dogs somewhere along the path to adoption. Some are being treated at veterinary clinics, some are in boarding, some with special medical needs are with special medical fosters, and others are in private homes. Only when a dog is deemed fully healthy and able to travel by a veterinarian will she send a dog north with Greg. With all the handling and driving of dogs she spends a lot of time cleaning.

"I do laundry three to four times a day," she tells me. And she has a car and crates to clean every day too. Most people, myself included, couldn't live this way, but it's the way many people committed to rescue tend to live. They're all in.

While Kathy takes a small number of dogs from the Forgotten Dogs of the Fifth Ward Project, like Tadpole, she mainly pulls from shelters such as the one in Harris County which serves the county outside Houston's city limits, and Houston's BARC.

In 2009, Nathan Winograd, a California attorney, founder of the No Kill Advocacy Center and a leader of the national no-kill movement, was retained by the city of Houston to assess BARC. In his 196-page report, he found BARC deficient in almost every imaginable respect: poor infection control, lax enforcement of health protocols, unmotivated, poorly trained staff, animals living in their own waste, an inadequate adoption program and little regard for customer relations that might help raise the adoption rate and lower the kill rate, poor record keeping, and even confusing, inconsistent signage to alert the public to the hours of operation. Not surprisingly, BARC's reputation as a high-kill, low-compassion facility was widespread both locally and in rescue circles nationally.

The morning after my foray with Kelle and Alicia into the Fifth Ward, Kathy has arranged for us to tour BARC with Mauricio Zepeda, BARC's adoption and volunteer coordinator.

"Mauricio is fabulous," Kathy tells me, "and BARC is doing a much better job at raising the adoption rate and with infection control. There's been almost an entire staff turnover in recent years; they're younger and they seem to care much more."

I have no expertise in shelter management, but as Mauricio leads us through the large facility — there are approximately 540 kennels for dogs and cats — it seems clean and well organized. Staff members appear busy cleaning kennels, managing the intake of new animals, and working with volunteers to get dogs out for exercise in newly constructed runs. Ground has been broken for a new and, importantly, separate adoption center on the property. Today, people coming to look at the animals available for adoption have to share the same busy waiting area as people surrendering animals or dropping off strays they've picked up, an environment that can be unpleasant, chaotic, and noisy. A separate, welcoming, customer-oriented adoption center should lift the adoption rate.

While the criticisms of BARC over the years have been many, much of it has focused on the euthanasia rate. In 2005, it was 80 percent. Over the past decade, the kill rate for dogs and cats has dropped. By 2010, it had dropped to 58 percent, to 56 percent in 2011, and 57 percent in 2012. In 2013, the rate was about 50 percent — still high, to be sure, but markedly better than a decade ago.

Judging a shelter's performance by its euthanasia rate alone isn't entirely fair, especially since there are animals euthanized for what most would consider legitimate health and safety reasons. Intakes, average lengths of stay, infection control protocols, and many other factors have to be considered. Of primary concern to animal welfare advocates is the euthanasia of healthy or treatable, adoptable animals. To address this, BARC has implemented the Asilomar Accords, developed at a conference of animal welfare leaders in 2004, to provide "a uniform system for collecting and reporting shelter data," according to the National

Federation of Humane Societies. The goal was to lower the euthanasia rate of healthy, treatable animals in shelters. Those accords emphasize the so-called "live release rate," which is calculated by taking all live outcomes and dividing it by all outcomes minus owner requested euthanasia for unhealthy or untreatable animals. But it's up to the judgment of individual shelters as to what constitutes unhealthy and untreatable. If the number of animals surrendered by owners and designated unhealthy/untreatable is inflated, the live release rate may be deceptively encouraging. Also not counted in determining the live release rate is the number of animals that died or were lost in shelter care. In 2013, there were 426 animals in that category at BARC.

Some groups, such as No Kill Houston, remain fierce critics, noting BARC killed 12,596 animals in 2013. While no one disputes there's always more that can be done to lower that rate — the new adoption center is such a step — the fact is Houston has an extraordinarily severe dog and cat overpopulation problem. As Alicia McCarty of Forgotten Dogs of the Fifth Ward Project said, it's a problem the city can't adopt its way out of.

"We have a great staff here now," Mauricio tells me. "A few years ago it was awful. BARC was a dumping ground not just for dogs and cats, but also for bad city employees."

Other improvements have been programmatic, such as the Healthy Pets, Healthy Streets Initiative, begun in 2012, which includes a mobile clinic where people can bring their pets and have them spayed or neutered for free and receive free vaccines, free dog and cat licenses, and free microchipping.

Kathy tells me Mauricio is very dedicated; she often gets email pleas he sends to various rescue groups at ten or eleven o'clock at night about animals who are down to their final hours.

As an "open intake" shelter, BARC has to take any animal for any reason, and it takes in about twenty-five thousand a year. The day before our visit BARC took in 150 animals.

"We're always over capacity," Mauricio tells me. Not only are hundreds of animals brought into BARC every week, but many are also left tied to the perimeter fences at night, and some are even dropped at employees' homes. "If people know you work at BARC," Mauricio says, "they'll just dump dogs or cats at your house."

To help with overcrowding, Mauricio has about 150 people who foster for BARC and can bring the animals there for basic veterinary care from one of the four staff veterinarians, and he has an outreach team that works with rescue groups to facilitate rescues and adoptions.

Mauricio seems to have a genuine love of animals; he has several dogs himself. But he's also part of the team making decisions about which animals will be euthanized, a team that comprises the chief veterinarian, the shelter manager, and himself. With so many animals coming in each week and finite space, "There's no choice," he says. "We can't become hoarders ourselves."

As Kathy and I leave BARC, I tell her my impressions: that it seems to have come a long way since Nathan Winograd's scathing 2009 report.

"BARC was a house of horrors eight years ago," Kathy says as she waves to the guard who opens the rear gate so we can drive out. "Almost no dogs got out. The staff is much better and they have a ton of volunteers who keep an eye on the staff."

The picture at the Harris County Shelter, where Kathy also pulls many dogs, is quite different.

The euthanasia rate there is about 80

percent, according to Kathy. "There's no volunteer base. They don't vaccinate on entry because they know they're going to kill so many and don't want to make the investment. It's an older, long-time staff up there and they have about 150 to 180 dogs at a time, two to three per cage. They clean the cages and feed them once a day. I've never seen a dog exercised there.

"The staff knows me, and they are nice to me, but the shelter is under the control of the county commissioners, a bunch of good ol' boys who just don't care," she tells me. "They're politicians. They only care when people complain about nuisances, but there's no concern for the dogs.

"People need to spend a day in a shelter in order to understand the problem and the suffering," she says as she parks her Land Rover near the restaurant where we'll have lunch. "Education about how to care for animals is key."

Kathy's iPhone is always lighting up with incoming messages, and over lunch she gets an email Mauricio has sent to dozens of rescue groups he works with regularly. It's a list, with pictures, of all the dogs to be euthanized at BARC later that day if they aren't adopted or rescued in the next few hours. On the list are many we saw just an hour ago, healthy, happy, adorable dogs who've reached the end of the line because there simply isn't any more room; scores of new dogs are arriving daily. Kathy gets at least one message like this, often more, from BARC daily.

Kathy emails another group, Rescue Pets Movement, which works with rescue organizations in Colorado to try and move dogs from Houston up there for adoption. She offers to pay the boarding costs for two dogs on the list, Billy, a black Lab mix and Lori, a yellow Lab mix, if Rescue Pets Movement will assume responsibility for them. It's shortly after noon. Mauricio will need a commitment by four o'clock if Billy and Lori are to be spared. Later in the afternoon, with the hours winding down, Rescue Pets Movement emails Kathy and says "yes."

Then another email comes in from Mauricio. While walking the kennels at BARC that morning, we saw a sweet yellow Lab mix lying quietly and sadly under a blanket in a kennel. She had arrived shortly before and was being treated for a serious injury, cause unknown. She was unable to bear weight on one of her front legs and had possible radial nerve damage and lameness in a rear leg. Healthy dogs have to be held at

BARC for seventy-two hours by law, time to give owners a chance to reclaim their dogs. But an earlier medical release to a foster or rescue organization is possible when a dog is sick or injured.

"Friendly dog, stable condition for now, available for foster or rescue on early medical release," says the email.

"Sometimes everyone is waiting for someone else to step up because we are all so overwhelmed," Kathy says. "And often it goes down to the last moment. Because she's injured, she can't be put up for adoption. If no one steps up to rescue or foster, she'll be put down." This poor dog also found a guardian angel: Red Collar Rescue of Houston.

After lunch we head to the offices of a veterinary ophthalmologist with Sunset, a two-year-old female Cairn terrier Kathy pulled from BARC two weeks earlier. Like nearly every dog Kathy pulls, Sunset came first to Kathy's home.

"It's rare [when] a dog can go immediately to foster," she tells me. "Almost every dog I pull comes home with me so I can evaluate their needs."

Sunset is heartworm positive, so before sending her to a foster, Kathy wants to see how extensive the treatment will be. But now we are attending to another problem; one of Sunset's eyes is clouded over.

"I get tired," Kathy tells me as we sit in traffic. "Most people doing rescue burn out after ten years. There are days when I think I can't do it anymore and then you see a dog in need and you can't say no. The dogs have no one to speak for them. It's not their fault."

For every ten adoption applications she receives at Houston Shaggy Dog Rescue, Kathy turns down about eight for various reasons. She thoroughly screens every potential adopter and has high standards. Her dogs have had enough hardship; she wants to be as sure as she can be about every match. If she learns from your veterinarian you were lax about some aspect of a previous pet's care, she's going to turn you down. If you're planning to leave the dog outdoors all the time, you aren't going to get one of Kathy's dogs. She catches a lot of flak from some she turns down, but it doesn't faze her. She's not interested in making every applicant happy; it's all about the dog being happy. "I'm the toughest rescue in the city to get a dog from," Kathy tells me. "People lie on applications all the time."

There's an ongoing debate in rescue circles about just how thorough the screening of potential adopters should be. Some argue that it's better to take a chance moving a dog to a new home, even one that's only been cursorily evaluated, or perhaps not evaluated at all, than to see it euthanized; others, like Kathy, are extremely rigorous. There are reasonable arguments on each side, but when it comes to a dog in which you have invested enormous time, energy, and money, it's perfectly understandable for Kathy to be as tough as she is. And no legitimate rescue wants to send a dog knowingly into a bad situation.

Growing up on a farm on the Isle of Wight, Kathy "rescued everything and anything that needed rescue," she tells me. "My first rescue was a baby owl with a crossed beak that had been kicked out of its nest. I took care of it until it was big enough to catch its own food, and that owl lived on our farm for many years. I was taught to have compassion for animals. All of my sisters feel the same way, and I have rescued animals all of my life. But what drives my passion in Houston is the plight of all of the dogs that are dumped on our streets and so many that are abused."

Kathy "fell into" canine rescue in Houston

without intending to. "Someone I met at a Starbucks saw me with my dog and we got to talking. She asked if I'd be interested in fostering a dog that was in bad shape and I agreed. I spent $2,000 getting it better and finding an adoptive home. I thought I'd try a couple of more dogs and found that I liked it, but it was getting expensive. That's when I decided to start a rescue and incorporate it as a nonprofit. My coworkers at the real estate office thought I was crazy.

"The first dog I rescued was Windsor, a shaggy black mutt," Kathy continues. "I went looking for a dog for a friend and saw Windsor who was absolutely terrified. I thought no one else would take him, so I did. I don't like to fail, but Windsor wrecked my house — the curtains, the furniture, everything. I had just redecorated. He even injured my ankle pulling me into a ditch. I sat on the floor and wondered, *What have I done?* But I wasn't going to take him back to the shelter. I found a trainer and a day care and he got better. People give up too early on dogs. They aren't willing to work with them. I see it in applications I get for my dogs all the time. People want hypoallergenic, non-shedding, no barking, good-with-kids dogs. They want perfect dogs. What they need is a stuffed animal. Windsor is fourteen now, and when I look for dogs, I think of Windsor and see dogs that seem unadoptable but who, with a little TLC, can be great, happy dogs."

The eye vet, Dr. J. F. Swanson, examines Sunset and notes she has no reflex response to light in her right eye. He thinks the eye suffered a traumatic injury, but it's not inflamed and there are no other symptoms. "The left eye is completely normal," he tells Kathy, "but she's completely blind in her right. It appears she's been this way for a while."

Importantly for Kathy, she now knows exactly what she's dealing with. Sunset will still be a completely adoptable dog once her heartworm is successfully treated; Kathy will just have to tell potential adopters she's blind in one eye and it requires no treatment.

Toward the end of the day, more emails start to pour in from BARC: final appeals for dogs about to be put down. This is the time of day when the animal control officers who have been picking up dogs pull into the intake bay and room needs to be made for the new arrivals.

"I hope I have a few more years left in rescue," Kathy says to me as she drives me back to my hotel. "It's really a younger person's endeavor with all the physical work. Just once I'd like to sleep in until six o'clock. It's like having kids who rely on you for everything. You can't let them down. They've been let down before and you can't do it again."

A few days after I returned home from Houston, I checked in with Kathy about Tadpole.

"He is doing great," she emailed me. "His coat is coming back. Hope I can get him out of isolation soon. He should be ready in September to be put up for adoption if all goes well."

I'm relieved and happy for him. The poor guy had received two ivermectin shots for his scabies, two dewormings, and all of his vaccines — for bordetella, lepto, distemper, parvo, and canine influenza — and two medicated baths. So there was hope after all.

But ten days later, Kathy wrote again. "I have some sad news," she began. "Tadpole passed away today. He got sick this weekend and would not eat and had very watery diarrhea. I took him to the vet and they said he was full of infection . . . his white blood cell count was practically zero and he had high positive parvo." Apparently, the parvo had been incubating since before his vaccine, so though Kathy did everything she could to try to save him, it was, sadly, a lost cause.[22]

She continued: "With no white blood cells, he could not fight the infection so we started plasma transfusions and IVs . . . but tonight when they were giving him his evening meds, he had a heart attack and died. It's so sad and we see this so much with the street dogs; [they] have no immune system built up . . . it's just hard to save them. He was such a sweet dog and loved his toys I bought him and to see [him] go that way and so fast is heartbreaking. Thank you for caring about him; hope he is in a better place than he came from.

"These are the days," she ended, "that make me question how much longer I can

22. Puppies require three parvo vaccines three weeks apart to be fully immunized. Tadpole had only his first and because Kathy kept him in isolation, he must have been exposed earlier. If a dog already has parvovirus in the body, the first vaccine won't usually protect or heal them, unfortunately. Because it can be costly to treat — Kathy had spent $900 for treatment before Tadpole died — and is highly contagious, many shelters, and even some rescues, will put puppies down as soon as they show symptoms of the disease.

do this."

But, knowing Kathy, I knew she'd be back at BARC tomorrow morning, looking for another shaggy dog to rescue.

7
HARD TIMES

The Brazoria County shelter in Texas is a tiny facility, maybe fifteen hundred square feet, with additional pens outside, and can accommodate a few dozen dogs. The land here is as flat as a pancake and bakes in the south Texas sun. When you walk on the nearby grass, you have to be careful where you stand. Pick the wrong spot and you'll be crawling with fire ants before you know it.

Some of the dogs Greg picks up in Baytown have been pulled from this shelter by Tom English, the mathematics professor I first met in Baytown while riding with Greg. On my return visit to Texas, after spending a few days in Houston with Kelle and Alicia and Kathy, I also spent some time with Tom observing his work near his home in Texas City.

Tom comes to the Brazoria County shelter once or twice a week. It's about a forty-five-

minute drive from Texas City, a refinery and chemical production city on Galveston Bay about forty miles from downtown Houston. The county has no food budget for the shelter, so Tom and other donors deliver food. And though he isn't a veterinarian, Tom also brings and administers vaccines. He has negotiated a volume discount from Schering-Plough, the major pharmaceutical company, and resells them, at his cost, to several shelters in southeast Texas. He also draws blood samples from each new arrival, which he ships to a lab to determine which dogs have heartworm, photographs each dog, and distributes the photos to a network of rescue groups. The Brazoria County shelter has no adoption program — it's too remote and too small — and if it did, it would be required by law to spay and neuter the adopted animals and has no facility for doing so.

But over the past few years, with Tom's help and a devoted county employee named Tammy Grable, the shelter secretary, the euthanasia rate here has dropped from about 80 percent to 20 percent. In June 2014, for example, of the 178 dogs and cats the shelter took in, 129 were taken by rescue organizations. Tom has also helped establish an intake protocol that has improved infection control at the facility. When animals arrive on the county's animal control vehicles, they are vaccinated for distemper, parvo, and bordetella, deflead, dewormed, and given a heartworm preventative before they enter the shelter. This means fewer dogs are put down for health reasons.

This small shelter has become a bright spot in the often-dark world of rescue: dogs who wind up here have a decent shot at getting out and finding a home. Indeed, later this week, seven dogs Tom has pulled from here will be traveling north with Greg, six to Rottie Empire Rescue in New York state and one to a forever home in Connecticut.

Today, the temperature is in the upper nineties with humidity to match. There's hardly a cloud in the sky and no nearby trees to offer shade. I'm wilting in the intense heat after driving here with Tom; his friend Vince, a fellow mathematician; and Jenni Hendricks of Southern Comforts Animal Rescue of Hitchcock, Texas, which adopts out about 150 to 200 dogs a year, primarily to the Northeast, from various shelters in southeast Texas.

Every day, seven days a week, Bobby Lee Richardson,[23] fifty-three, walks about a hundred yards from where he lives to this shelter to take care of the dogs. Mr. Richardson, as I call him, is wearing what he wears to work at the shelter every day: loose-fitting orange pants tied at the waist and an olive T-shirt with a name tag sewn above the left breast. His silver hair is cropped close and his neck, arms and strong-featured face are nearly black from the sun. A sharp Texas twang inflects his words. But the most interesting thing about Mr. Richardson isn't his twang or his appearance, but where he lives and what he does. Just a stone's throw away is the Brazoria County jail, where he's serving a fifteen-year sentence for driving under the influence, his fifth DUI offense.

23. This is a pseudonym.

After we unload the food we're delivering, Tom begins the process of photographing each dog, taking blood samples, clipping nails where needed, and examining gums to estimate their age. Mr. Richardson fetches each new dog from its kennel and offers his own assessment of its temperament, which is important for Tom to know before he pokes it with a needle for the blood draw. That way Tom will know if a dog is likely to be docile or a potential biter. I'm awed by Mr. Richardson's care and knowledge of the dogs: he's very tender with them, has great empathy for them, and is a keen observer of their personalities.

The first is a young boxer whose left rear leg is swollen from an attack by a pit bull in the kennel they briefly shared three days earlier. Next is a Chow Chow mix suffering from flea dermatitis. One at a time, Mr. Richardson brings them from their kennels and Tom and Jenni go to work in the withering heat. Only one of the dogs seems too frightened to have his blood drawn, a bulldog mix, so Mr. Richardson places a towel over his head and holds him firmly while Tom inserts the needle in a foreleg.

Getting good photographs is key; a photo showing a dog at his or her best can mean the difference between rescue and euthanasia. In this case, looks do matter: Tom places most of these dogs with other rescue organizations and the photograph is the most important factor in their decision whether to take a dog because it will likely be an important factor for potential adopters. As Tom coaxes one of the dogs, a white pit bull, to look at the camera, a crop duster buzzes the fields behind him. Despite the heat, Tom keeps at it until he has the shot he wants of each of the two-dozen or so dogs.

"I'm a taxpayer," Mr. Richardson offers during a short break, perhaps his way of telling me not to write him off as nothing more than an alcoholic and a felon. After seeing him with the dogs, I know there's a lot more to this mysterious man than meets the eye. "I have two kids in college. One in San Antonio wants to be a history teacher. I did hydro testing for chemical plant pipes. I was in my third year when I got arrested again. I started drinking when I was in the military and I've been in trouble ever since."

He's working under the supervision of the sheriff's deputy, Amanda Kaylor, who's in charge of the shelter. She's a short, no-nonsense, cowboy-boot and dungaree-wearing woman with a pistol on her hip, a squint in her eyes, and a cigarette in her hand. But she trusts him enough to leave him to his work while she drives off for about fifteen minutes in her government-issued pickup truck to run an errand.

"They used to give each dog seventy-two hours," Mr. Richardson tells me as he cuddles an eight-week-old pit bull mix covered with fire ant bites. "The freezers were full of dogs. I know each dog, which are friendly, and which will get you. But I've never been gotten.

"He's my little baby," he coos to the puppy.

I'm not sure what freezers he's referring to but assume somewhere on the premises, or perhaps at the prison, euthanized dogs were kept in freezers until their bodies could be disposed of. The image is an awful one.

I also have no way of knowing how much of what Mr. Richardson has to say is accurate, and his accent is so thick I'm not even following it all. Still, whatever his crimes or flaws, I'm taken by his affection for the dogs.

Three of the dogs Tom is sending north with Greg in a few days are four-and-a-half-month-old Plott hound mix puppies that came from this shelter. Mr. Richardson would walk them every night around a small lake next to the prison and thought they were special. Tom took them home and arranged for Rottie Empire Rescue to take them.[24]

When the work is done, and everyone has sweated through their T-shirts, we take a look at a litter of puppies, no more than ten days old, and their mama, a black mouth cur mix, brought in over the weekend. The pups and their mama were found in a culvert pipe, and when sheriff's deputies couldn't get them out a woman who lives nearby used a pool net to reach them. Each puppy is wearing a green plastic collar with a number to tell them apart, but Mr. Richardson points out to Tom that the collars are irritating the mother as the puppies push against her to nurse. And puppies grow fast and the collars could quickly become too tight. He sees no point in the collars — at this age they don't need to be told apart — and Tom agrees. After checking with the deputy on duty, Tom cuts the collars off.

"It's extremely rare for a shelter to allow volunteers to do everything we do here," Tom says.

24. The name aside, Rottie Empire Rescue accepts breeds other than Rottweilers.

■ ■ ■ ■

Tom English is in his late forties, with brown hair and a sturdy build. In recent years he's devoted less time to pulling dogs for adoption and more working to improve the lives of dogs in the Brazoria County shelter and on the streets of some of the poorer areas of Galveston County. He initially approached the Galveston County shelter about working with them, but they weren't interested, so he moved on to neighboring Brazoria. A native of Erie, Pennsylvania, he attended graduate school in New York state and came to Texas City in 1998, leaving a lectureship at the University of Miami to teach at College of the Mainland, a two-year community college serving Galveston County.

"I was here for a few years before I realized there was a huge animal overpopulation problem," he tells me sitting at a table on the deck overlooking an expansive yard where the dozens of dogs he keeps, some permanent, some fosters, can roam. "My neighbor and I each had two Rottweilers and one night, it was 2005, he said to me, 'A Rottie was picked up by animal control outside your house the other night.' I thought someone had lost a dog and went to the local shelter to see if I could help reunite the dog and its owner. I was overwhelmed. The shelter was dingy, damp, and stinky and had no windows. It was overcrowded with dogs coughing and wheezing, and with runny eyes and ears. I left that day with four dogs: two more Rotties and two Lab mixes. I adopted three of them and still have Gertrude, the lost Rottweiler my neighbor told me about."

Tom then tried working with a local rescue group, but found it dysfunctional and ineffective. He later connected with a New Hampshire–based rescue, For the Love of Dog, which was trying to save three Rottweilers in Houston. As his passion for canine rescue grew, his romantic life suffered.

"I had a girlfriend at the time, but the stress of rescue work and the number of dogs in the house led to our breakup," he tells me. At the time of my visit, he was in a new relationship with a woman, Lisa, who seemed as passionate about dogs as he is.

"Three or four years ago, I started Nutmeg Rescue with a woman from Connecticut," he continues. "It was ad hoc, not incorporated. I was sort of a freelance rescuer placing dogs through many other organizations such as Labs4rescue, Mutts4rescue, For Love of Dog, and Rottie Empire Rescue. I've placed more than two thousand dogs over the years."

About fifteen hundred of those dogs traveled north with Greg Mahle. Many others, mostly smaller breeds and puppies, flew north through Continental Airlines' PetSafe program, essentially air travel for dogs.

"In rescue we all use the *Sophie's Choice* analogy," he explains regretfully, referring to the William Styron novel in which a woman, caught in the Holocaust, is forced by the Nazis to choose whether her son or daughter will be spared. "Who lives and who dies? Adoptability is a huge criterion in saving a dog. You want dogs that will be adopted quickly so you can save another. It's a numbers game. How do you save the greatest number?"

Tom believes the overwhelming scale of the overpopulation problem makes euthanasia inevitable.

"If you don't euthanize dogs, you get dogs piled up on top of dogs," he explains, realizing his view isn't popular with many in rescue, especially those firmly committed to the no-kill philosophy. "You get a disease-filled facility where you can't keep up with the cleaning and the feeding. Even a healthy, adoptable dog in such a facility will live a horrible life if it doesn't find a home and [has to] stay in the facility. Some go crazy and turn on one another. I am supportive of 'no suffering' rather than 'no kill.' Then we can try and go from no suffering to no kill. I don't want dogs dying of disease in a shelter. Better to die by needle than flea anemia. You just can't jump right to no kill, but I support it as an aspiration."

After several years, he burned out on rescue and switched his focus from adoptions to what he calls "shelter and community support."

"I can go out and rescue dogs willy-nilly, but it doesn't change the big picture," he says. "So I looked for situations I could turn around, whether a particular shelter, such as Brazoria, or a community, such as San Leon, where we're going tomorrow. At Brazoria they almost never euthanize a healthy, adoptable dog anymore. That's where doing my part has made a difference."

I ask Tom if there was anything in his early life experience that triggered his passion for canine rescue.

"I was a fat, shy kid with few friends," he tells me. "When I was eight, we adopted a dog from the Erie shelter and he became my best friend. His name was Midnight, a thirty-five pound shepherd mix. We were so attached. He was smart and special, and it impressed me that he was a thinking, feeling being. It got imprinted in my mind that dogs are not disposable.

"There is an addictive component to rescue," Tom continues. "You get a high rescuing a dog that's been living in a shelter and you bathe it and care for it and see it running in the yard. You get addicted to that feeling." Greg said much the same to me on several occasions: he does what he does, he told me, "because it feels so good."

Jenni Hendricks of Southern Comforts Animal Rescue agrees. "Rescue is addictive," she says. "You want to take a break and clean up your house, but the phone rings and it's about a puppy and you're on your way."

"Dogs are like children at their very best age," Tom continues. "They look up to you. They adore you. They want to be with you. Lots of people in rescue don't have children and the dogs become a substitute. I wanted to have kids at some point, but it didn't happen. And if I spend $30,000 a year on the dogs, it's a bargain because I'm doing what I love. How many people get to do that? Rescue people will have no trouble spending $1,000 on a dog, but they won't spend

249

$30 on a pair of shoes.

"Because you can only save a relative few, you get beaten down again and again," he muses. "You lose much more than you win. But you keep going. How can you not feel defeated coming back from a shelter? I don't know what's going to happen to any of those dogs we saw this morning. I post the pictures and hope rescues will contact the shelter and pull them. But I don't follow up because I don't want to know. There are a lot of crappy rescues out there, but you hope for the best for each one."

After we had returned from the Brazoria County shelter, I helped Tom move some lumber he'd cut to make eight wooden pallets. Tomorrow we'll deliver the pallets to give eight dogs a space a few inches above the ground where they can stay dry when the dirt yards they live in turn to muck in the rain.

The next morning, with the pallets loaded into a large white van Tom bought specifically for his rescue work, we head off, with Vince, to pick up Sarah Manns in nearby San Leon, a community on Galveston Bay northeast of Texas City. Sarah and one helper comprise Companion Animal Outreach of Galveston County, an effort to improve the lives of neglected and mal-treated dogs in San Leon. Tom has agreed to lend a hand. This is what he means when he speaks of "community support" work, also known as "embedded animal welfare"; it's what Kelle and Alicia of the Forgotten Dogs of the Fifth Ward Project do in Houston.

House by house, block by block, Sarah is trying to help the countless yard dogs living in squalor, many next to tin-can trailers on trash-strewn lots in San Leon and neighboring Bacliff. Like Houston's Fifth Ward, this is an area of extreme poverty and it seems there's a dog, typically a pit bull mix, chained to a metal post in every yard.

One of those dogs, a one-year-old pit bull named Gauge, has become tangled in his chain and can move only a few feet, unable to reach his only water source, a kiddie pool filled with fetid water. There is no sign of the owners. In the hot Texas sun, those chains can become hot to the touch if there's no shade. Today, the heat index is well over one hundred degrees; there will be stretches here where the heat index will be in triple digits for weeks on end. Gauge seems starved for affection and is overjoyed to see Sarah and feel her touch as she and Vince work to untangle his chain. Gauge is one of the dogs getting a pallet today.

"When they're young, they're very affectionate when strangers come by, but after years on a chain, he'll eventually become nonsocial," Sarah explains.

"You do what you can in small steps to earn people's trust and try and help them become responsible pet owners," Tom tells me as we drive the neighborhood with Sarah. "You can't just lecture them and tell them what they're doing wrong. We're just trying to give these dogs out here a reasonable existence. If you take a dog away they just get another dog that's condemned to the same kind of life."

At one tiny trailer, in a yard filled with debris including thousands of sharp oyster shells, there are two chained dogs that become excited when they see us. They run back and forth as far as their chains will allow. Sarah says the trailer's occupants are mentally ill; either they're not home or decide not to venture out when we approach. A bag of dry dog food she delivered last week sits unopened by the trailer door. A case of canned food sits in the hot sun, also untouched. As Vince places a pallet near one of the dogs, Sarah gives the dog a treat and some affection.

In another yard, a forlorn pit bull mix

puppy, Diva, just four months old, lies against a tree, tethered to a line running above and across the yard. Many of these dogs will live their entire lives chained to a spike or a fence, never knowing the joy of running through a field, the softness of a carpeted floor, or a dip in a cool lake or stream.

"There's a lot of drugs out here, gang bangers and meth heads," Sarah says. "Few people here work. They party all night and sleep all day. The dogs serve as alarm systems for many of these people. Some of these dogs are chained up for *years.*

"There are also a lot of transients here, which makes it hard to help some of the dogs," she adds. "Sometimes I tell people to give me a week and I'll come back with vaccines, heartworm medications, and food, and when I come back they're gone. Parvo is rampant. People's dogs have pups, and they move place to place, leaving the infection behind for the next dog that moves in." There are also backyard breeders in the neighborhood, breeding dogs behind trailers in grounds littered with parvo.

Week after week, Sarah comes out here providing food, food bowls, toys, and small store-bought shelters for dogs in need. In return, she tries to secure agreements from the owners to get their dogs spayed or neutered.

"I hate it here because of the way people treat animals," Sarah tells me as we drive through Bacliff. She's a California native who moved here from Alaska. Right along the bay, there are some expensive homes, but nearly every street we drive down is lined with dilapidated trailers, yards strewn with trash, junked cars and old tires, chain-link fences, and dogs chained to posts. In one, a dog on a short chain is defecating into a water bowl. "As soon as I moved here and saw all the stray cats at an apartment complex I managed, I started doing animal welfare work."

Like the Fifth Ward in Houston, local government seems to have washed its hands of the people and animals that live, and die, on these streets.

"Dead dogs lie in the street for days," Sarah tells me, "and get bloated in the sun. You call the town agencies and they just kick you from one to the other and no one will come and pick up the dog.

"For a long time I bought all the food myself," Sarah tells me. "Now I get it through a rescue food bank, and I get some support from local groups, such as the Animal Alliance, but I still finance most of this work out of my own pocket." Nevertheless, she's not always welcome in the neighborhood. "Some people will hug you, but I also get cussed out and spit on too."

By the end of the morning, after spending a few hours in San Leon and Bacliff, I felt like I'd fallen through a rabbit hole into a world I neither recognized nor wanted to ever see again, a world of desperate people and desperate dogs, a hopeless place where a few people, such as Tom English and Sarah Manns, try to change a handful of lives for the better.

Yet, it's a world other people need to see too. And not just to understand the plight of these dogs, so they'll hopefully "think rescue" if they ever decide to get a dog of their own, but the plight of these people. There's much talk these days about the growing inequality between rich and poor, but places like Houston's Fifth Ward and San Leon, which sits near the nation's largest oil and gas refineries, bring that issue to the forefront. In these places filled with hopeless people and hopeless dogs living very hopeless lives, it's hard to find any evidence of the American dream. But what you can find are people like Tom and Sarah and Jenni, chipping away at a tiny piece of the problem with true American spirit.

By bedtime, I would be back in my comfortable home outside of Boston. I wanted nothing more than to see Albie, curl up with him on the bed, and rub his very lucky belly.

8
ACADIANA

In the last two chapters, we returned to Houston, Brazoria County, and San Leon to better understand how some of the dogs Greg boards in Baytown happened to be at his door that hot afternoon when Kathy Wetmore left us with Willis, the world's happiest dog, and a feast from Whole Foods. I also returned to Lafayette Parish where, the morning after loading Keri's dogs in Alexandria, and the pick-ups in Baytown, we would board fifteen additional dogs headed north. I wanted to spend more time at Lafayette Animal Aid (LAA) in Carencro, where Greg picks up dogs on each trip, because it's a very different operation than Keri's in Alexandria or Kathy's in Houston or Tom's in and around Texas City.

Lafayette Parish is part of a large swath of south-central and southwestern Louisiana known as Acadiana or, more popularly, Cajun Country. The descendants of

eighteenth-century exiles from the region that comprises Canada's maritime provinces, many Cajuns speak a French dialect, but the area is ethnically diverse; it's a mix of Cajuns, Native Americans, Creoles (native-born Louisianans often of mixed ancestry), Germans, and, more recently, Southeast Asians.

During my travels, I often heard rescue people say, "If I won the lottery . . ." followed by a wish list of what they need to help the dogs. In Greg's case, it would be a new tractor and trailer, but for the others, those pulling dogs from shelters and rescuing them off the streets, at the top of the list is always a piece of land where they would build a well-equipped, comfortable shelter, so they could rescue more dogs and have a proper place to put them: no more patching together a network of fosters; no more running from place to place, moving dogs from here to there; no more living in their own homes with dozens of dogs because they've run out of other options. If they had their dreams fulfilled, what they'd have would look a lot like LAA.

Set on ten acres of land, LAA's main shelter building is a rescuer's dream. Five thousand nine hundred square feet of bright, clean kennels for cats and dogs, medical treatment rooms, and storage and office space. There's a separate heated and air-conditioned cottage dedicated solely to the comfort of "sanctuary" cats (about three-dozen cats that for various reasons will live their lives here), a six-thousand-square-foot barn for both equipment storage and isolation facilities for animals that have, or may have, contagious diseases, and large, shaded, fenced spaces for dogs to run and play in.

Just about to open on the property when I visited was a new veterinary clinic, a triple-wide trailer that had served as a nearby general practitioner's office. When he retired, he donated it to LAA, and it had been towed to the property. LAA invested $20,000 to ready it for its own use. The nearly two-thousand-square-foot building comprises three exam rooms, an operating room, a recovery room, offices, a supply room, a bathroom with shower, a laundry room, and a kitchen.

LAA has thirteen paid staff, five full-time and eight part-time, and a bevy of volunteers. Just an hour and half south of Alexandria where Keri Toth, Greta Jones, and Sara Kelly scramble every day to hold together a heroic rescue effort with gumption, passion, and endless improvisation despite a dearth of financial resources, LAA is institutionalized rescue in the best sense of the word: a professional staff, an active board of directors, excellent facilities, and money in the bank.

How has LAA been able to pull this off while so many other rescue organizations struggle? LAA is the legacy of the late Miriam Weiss, a Lafayette native whose third husband was a New York City judge she met while vacationing on Long Island. She kept a home in Lafayette and ran a family business there, an upscale women's clothing

store. Later in her life, she returned to Lafayette, donated the land, and built the
shelter, completed shortly before she died
in 2005, at a cost of $750,000. In her will,
she left a significant bequest in trust to the
organization. The income from the trust
finances about a quarter of its half-million-
dollar-a-year operating budget. The rest
comes from donations and grants. If necessary, LAA can tap the trust principal. It's a
luxury relatively few rescues enjoy — so is a
paid staff.

"It's hard when rescue organizations rely
strictly on volunteers," Melinda Falgout,
LAA's board president, tells me. "With a
staff, you can be much more efficient and
ensure you can carry on even when people
leave. Investing in staff will help us continue
to grow. Beyond rescue, we want to make a
big impact on public education and public
policy."

One public policy priority is stepping up
enforcement of the state's often-ignored
animal cruelty laws. The LAA board has one
attorney member and Melinda is hoping to
create a legal advisory board. On the education front, another LAA board member, a
teacher by profession, runs a reading program for second graders called I Read to
Animals. The children read books about

261

rescue dogs such as *Buddy Unchained* and *Before You Were Mine,* books with strong messages of responsible pet ownership. They read aloud to a therapy dog named Cece, a golden retriever who belongs to Melinda and her husband, Gary. Each child signs a pledge to care for animals and receives a gift certificate for pet food and a stuffed animal. The program started in the Lafayette public schools, then expanded to the schools in Saint Martin Parish.

In addition to an executive director and a staff veterinarian, the LAA staff comprises four kennel workers, a cat director and three cat workers, an adoption coordinator, a development director, and an administrative assistant who manages intakes, phones, and email. On an average day, LAA receives about thirty calls to take in animals. New arrivals from local shelters, or those without a medical history, are isolated for a week from the general population to minimize the risk of infectious disease, and all are started on their basic vaccine regimen. More than 75 percent of the dogs test heartworm positive on intake and are treated before being put up for adoption. LAA also operates a pet food bank for local residents who need food assistance, distributing about $25,000 worth of food a year.

But even a modern shelter like this one, built to accommodate about seventy-five dogs, is often over capacity, given the scope of the canine overpopulation problem here, so LAA relies on about a dozen regular fosters, including Melinda and other board members, to take in dogs temporarily while they await adoption. There's also a full-time foster coordinator.

Volunteers walk each dog five times a day — careful records are kept of who has been out, when, for how long, and with whom — and there is an enrichment manual to guide the process of socializing each dog and making sure boredom is kept to a minimum. Dogs that remain in shelters with little socialization can develop behavioral problems that can render them unadoptable, so each new dog is matched with a volunteer to socialize them and provide enrichment throughout their stay.

On the first day of my visit to LAA, as I walked back to the main building after touring the cat cottage, I saw a group of staff and volunteers gathered in the cemetery on the premises, a lush lawn surrounded by an attractive wooden fence and lined with perennial gardens, where animals that die while in residence can be given a dignified burial. Some may come in seriously injured or very ill; some, for various reasons, live out their natural lives here. On a rare occasion, an animal is euthanized when there's consensus among the executive director, a PhD in cognitive science, Carley Faughn; Shannon Landry, the staff veterinarian; and Melinda, the board president, that the animal's quality of life is so compromised that euthanasia is the only humane option.

After the funeral, back in the main shelter building, Shannon and Carley, with a small assist from me, work to get dogs ready for transport. Greg will be here again the day after tomorrow and there's a lot to be done: each dog needs to be weighed, micro-chipped, and, depending on age, given various vaccines. The recently spayed and neutered pups need to have their stitches removed. Shannon checks their hearts and breathing with her stethoscope, looks in their ears and at their gums, checks for fleas, takes their temperature, and does a fecal exam. All of this is needed to complete the interstate travel certificate Greg needs for each dog on board. This time around, there will be twenty-four dogs from LAA going north with Greg, twice as many we loaded a few weeks ago when I first passed through with him.

Among them are two dachshund–basset hound puppies, Pilsner and Wheat, light brown with short legs, huge ears, and phlegmatic, wise-beyond-their-years demeanors. Their mama, Abita (named after the Louisiana-brewed brand of beer), is also making the trip, all bound for forever homes. Also traveling are seven precious heeler mix puppies, each patient and calm in my hands as Shannon removes their stitches. Bound for a new home in New York is Sunflower, a beautiful yellow Lab mix with an old bone break on her right rear leg and buckshot in her body, pulled from the Saint Landry Parish Animal Shelter just north of here.

As soon as the dogs leave with Greg, the staff can begin pulling other dogs from area shelters, dogs with short leases on life that can take the spaces newly opened by those who have departed. Every dog that gets on board is a victory, and every one creates an opportunity for another deserving dog searching for a forever home.

On the second day of my visit to Lafayette, Melinda, April Reeves, LAA's adoption coordinator, and I drive about half an hour to the Saint Martin Parish Animal Services shelter, where LAA pulls many of its dogs.

Four years ago, a new shelter director was hired, Michelle Brignac, and the euthanasia rate has plummeted from close to 90 percent to below 20 percent, one of the lowest in the state. Had Bijou, the beagle mix, been in this shelter four years ago instead of a few weeks ago, his chances of getting out alive would have been slim. Today, he's living happily with his forever family outside of Boston.

Jamie Clark was born and raised in nearby Broussard, Louisiana, and returned there with her husband, also named Jamie, when he left the army in 2001. She spends a lot of time at the Saint Martin shelter, as a volunteer, pulling dogs for Lafayette Animal Aid and the Saint Martin Humane Society, and working closely with Michelle to move as many dogs as possible to other rescue organizations both in and out of state.

She was introduced to rescue shortly after returning to Broussard, when she read about a pit bull fighting ring that had been busted. The fighting dogs and the so-called "bait" dogs — defenseless dogs or dogs confined in some way so other dogs can attack it — were brought to the Saint Martin shelter. A public appeal went out looking for volunteers to foster the dogs that could be safely fostered. Jamie went to the shelter, thinking she'd take one home.

"I left with nine seven-day-old puppies born to one of the bait dogs," she tells me. "They tried to save the mother, but she'd been shot by the people running the fighting ring. So I rescued the puppies, thinking the shelter would help me find homes for them. But I was on my own and I started calling all the rescues in the area and put up posters at PetSmart.[25] The poster is how I first connected with the Saint Martin Humane Society, and we eventually found homes for all of them."

After working with the Saint Martin Humane Society for several years, Jamie realized local adoptions couldn't possibly keep pace with the number of dogs in need of homes, and she began exploring the options for local rescue groups and shelters to send dogs to out-of-state rescue organizations that might be able to find homes in their locations. Unburdened by the individual adoption process, rescue-to-rescue efforts allow greater numbers of dogs to escape high-kill shelters. But you have to be selective both about the dogs and the other rescue groups: you only want to send highly adoptable dogs and only to rescue organiza-

25. PetSmart is a national pet supply retailer.

tions you know will make every effort to work with dogs that need socialization, and find homes for them. Jamie knows some rescue groups have open adoption policies — meaning the adopters are not vetted — but when you know a dog is going to die within hours if it isn't transferred, she believes it's a risk you sometimes have to take.

Jamie's networking led her to Loving Friends Transport, a Florida-based animal transport service owned and operated by Laura Fletcher-Taylor and her husband, Jim Taylor. Now, Loving Friends Transport picks up dogs at Saint Martin Animal Control once a month. As it happens, its ultramodern tractor-trailer is idling in another heavy downpour outside as Jamie and I speak. The dogs will be delivered to the humane societies of Tampa, Sarasota, and Pinellas County. Because those organizations will spay and neuter them before finding homes, it makes life easier for Jamie and Michelle. They can move more dogs through the system at less cost without having to euthanize them to make room for new arrivals.

The Humane Society of Tampa adopts out about six thousand animals a year, and has full-time veterinarians on staff and the resources to take many dogs from other states. Though Florida also has a canine overpopulation problem, it takes highly adoptable out-of-state dogs: puppies, small breeds, healthy dogs — dogs that "fly off the shelf so to speak," according to Jamie. "Still, there are many, many highly adoptable dogs here they can't take, but every bit helps.

"When you have a director willing to expand the effort to rescue and transport, it makes all the difference," Jamie tells me. "This shelter used to have a terrible reputation and the euthanasia rate was sky-high. Michelle has reached out to rescue groups everywhere and created a network of fosters that allows us to take in more dogs and save more dogs. But as your live release rate goes up, so does your intake, so you become a victim of your own success."

Michelle has a business background, which she has used to her advantage. "Michelle stretches her budget in creative ways and has advocated for budget increases with the parish," says Jamie. "She has only two part-time employees and two part-time trustees from the local jail to help her here, and her salary is half of what many parish shelter directors make. She does so much more with less. Her attitude is she wants to save every dog. She sees every dog as an individual and is open to any new ideas to help us do that. She's built a big foster network. She even pulls dogs from other shelters with more resources and gets them on Loving Friends Transport out of her own budget. She's the model other shelter directors should be looking at."

For her part, Michelle thinks every animal control director, no matter how large or small a community they serve, could replicate what she's done.

"It's not about thinking outside the box," Michelle tells me. "There is no box. There's no limit to what you can do."

Turning the euthanasia rate around is harder in a small parish such as Saint Martin, she says: the budget is smaller (her department and the parish public health department share a budget of just over $100,000 annually); the shelter is small, so animals can't be held long; and there's a smaller population from which to find adopters.

Michelle started working at the Saint Martin shelter as a part-time employee cleaning kennels. Her background was in big-box retail with Walmart and Sears, but following a battle with cancer, she was looking for something else. She thinks it's been an advantage she didn't come up through the system as a professional animal control officer. When she was offered the directorship, she had to learn the job on her own: she understood management but, other than her own pets, had no training in animal care. She sought advice from veterinarians and rescue groups. Importantly, she wasn't an apprentice to her predecessor, so no one was there to tell her what *couldn't* be done.

For example, for 2015 the parish has budgeted $5,000 for animal euthanasia and zero for transport or outreach to rescue groups. Since no one has told her she can't reallocate funds as she sees fit, some of the money will be put toward life-saving efforts rather than euthanasia. Other shelter directors she's spoken with say they can't reallocate funds. And since no one has told her she can't fundraise for the shelter, she holds fundraising events and solicits support from individuals and local businesses to supplement her budget.

"I'd rather ask for forgiveness than permission," Michelle tells me, an attitude that has opened up a world of possibilities beyond business as usual.

"I know a handful of animal control directors who really want to do what's in the best interests of the animals," Michelle tells me.

271

"But more don't want to buck the system. They want to do their job and leave. But it's not just a job. You have to see it as more. There are lives at stake. These animals depend on you. You have to change the way you look at it. If you see it as just a job, you should get another job. It's appalling to me when I talk to other directors and I hear, 'I don't have the time,' or 'I can't do it that way.' Make the time. It can be done. These are just excuses. I do what I do because the animals can't do it for themselves. I want to be a facilitator for a better life for them, not the grim reaper."

When Michelle took over as director, no rescue groups were pulling from the shelter. Michelle has forged good relationships with many rescues. "I work with rescues to save more lives," she tells me. "I'm honored to work with rescue groups. We help each other."

Still, Jamie Clark worries that at some point Michelle will suffer "compassion fatigue," as so many other shelter directors do. Over the years, the job grinds them down and becomes a routine, and because people working in shelters see so many damaged dogs, it can become overwhelming if you can't compartmentalize.

But for now, Michelle remains undaunted.

"We had a Chihuahua, Penny, come in here recently that would have been euthanized almost immediately at any other shelter," Jamie tells me. "Someone had put a safety pin through her eye and eyelid and some kind of chemical in the other. She was the most flea-infested dog I've ever seen. Her nails were so long and her muscles so atrophied, we were sure she'd been kept in a small cage a long time. She was just a mess. Yet despite the terrible abuse she'd suffered, when we approached her, she just started wagging her tail. She should have been biting us, but she just wanted to love us. Michelle just couldn't put her down. Now she's at Lafayette Animal Aid getting ready for adoption."

Jamie has been offered more than one job as a shelter director, but she knows she could never do the part of the job the sheer number of dogs flooding the state's shelters requires: euthanizing an animal.

"Michelle has a very high compassion level," explains Jamie, "but she's able to do the most difficult part of the job. We can't save them all yet. But every animal has a good chance of leaving Saint Martin Parish shelter; at most others, they don't. I cry when I leave here. Working with Michelle has been such a blessing."

Jamie bemoans the treatment of dogs in her native Louisiana and offers an example.

"There are these hunting camps near Sabine where hunters come and their dogs wander around and reproduce," she tells me. "Hunting dogs are very disposable here. A lot of hunters believe for the dogs to hunt well, you have to starve them, make sure they're hungry. At the end of hunting season, the shelters see a noticeable increase in the number of Labs and other hunting dogs. One guy came to the shelter to dump his dog and was furious because he'd paid $1,200 for the dog and it had missed a duck. Another guy brought in a dog that had been riding in his pickup truck, fell out, and was badly hurt. His upper leg bone protruding from his shoulder."

Governor Jindal had vetoed the bill that would have required dogs riding in the back of pickup trucks to be properly secured a few weeks before Jamie and I spoke. Louisiana's animal cruelty statutes were enough, he said. But it was a common complaint among people doing rescue work in Louisiana that enforcement of animal cruelty laws is a low priority.

"In Vermillion Parish, there was a case of a breeder with three hundred dogs, and video evidence of dogs there with broken bones, dogs dying from exposure to the elements, and neither the sheriff nor the DA would take action," Jamie tells me. "And the shelter there won't work with rescue groups and doesn't do adoptions."

"Dogs here are property," April Reeves adds. "Even some of my own family members are appalled at what I do. Why would you do that for a dog?"

The following day, Melinda arranged for us to have lunch with Virginia Lee, supervisor of the Lafayette Animal Control shelter — where about half of all of LAA's rescue dogs come from — and tour the shelter. A former police officer in the city of Lafayette, Virginia is secretary of the Louisiana Animal Control Association, a professional association of the state's shelter directors.

Over hamburgers and fries at a local eatery, Virginia seems forthright about the problems afflicting the state's companion animals and shelters.

"I don't see things changing in my lifetime," Virginia tells me, referring to state's overpopulation problem. "I have seen some changes, but we need drastic changes.

"Getting dogs out of the shelter is our biggest challenge," she continues. Virginia herself adopted a schnauzer that came into the shelter. "We have way too many animals. Cats don't move; we'll always have a high euthanasia rate for cats. When it comes to direct adoptions of dogs, each dog we adopt out is micro-chipped, spayed or neutered, vaccinated, and dewormed. Our contract requires new owners take the dog to the veterinarian within a week. But I can't vet adopters as thoroughly as a rescue group can."

"We get between two and three thousand dogs in per year," says Virginia. "Ten years ago, it was more like five thousand, and the euthanasia rate was 90 percent. SpayNation [the Lafayette-based group that picked up a group of Keri's dogs in Alexandria] has helped lower the rate."

Virginia puts the canine euthanasia rate today at 55 percent. Of the dogs leaving the shelter alive, about a third are direct adoption, a third are returns to owner, and a third go to rescue groups, such as LAA.

"We have to put some dogs down because of overcrowding," adds Virginia. "Dogs are generally held for five days, though aggressive dogs go sooner. We make choices. We try to save good, adoptable dogs. If a rescue such as LAA identifies a dog they want, we'll hold it as long as we can and as long as we have space, typically a couple of weeks if they can't take the dog right away. We have room for about a hundred dogs and we're always at capacity. We euthanize every day to keep the flow going. It's awful doing the euthanasia. It's my least favorite part of my job."

Virginia contends her staff loves animals, which makes euthanizing them painstaking. Animals are sedated intravenously then killed using a heart stick.

"Making the choices and carrying it out wrenches your heart, and I won't lie to you, sometimes I miss," she says, referring to directing the heart stick precisely. "I don't think anyone really knows how many cats and dogs are euthanized in the state every year. There are so many small shelters, shelters without computers, and no state-wide collection of the information that does exist." She thinks the Humane Society of the United States' estimate of ninety thousand dogs and cats euthanized in Louisiana annually is probably low.

Virginia says transports bringing dogs north, such as Rescue Road Trips, are the best option for lowering the euthanasia rate. Stricter spay and neuter laws, and stricter laws governing treatment of animals are unlikely, she says, "because of the mentality here." And it takes resources and political will to enforce animal welfare laws and there's little public clamor for it. "Good laws do work if you have the people to enforce them," she says. "If we had a strong spay/neuter law and enforced it, things would change fast."

Like nearly everyone else I spoke to in Louisiana, Virginia thinks only education will provide a long-term answer.

"Ignorance is the problem here," Virginia continues. "There's no value in the ownership of an animal. Our rescue groups are doing a lot of education and in some portion of the population, that attitude has changed.

"Some animal control supervisors in the state don't see rescue organizations as allies," Virginia adds as she finishes her hamburger. "Some think rescues are filled with crazy people who love animals too much. Some think the rescues are just out to make money.[26] We certify [the] rescues we allow to pull from our shelter to be sure

26. From everything I saw and learned in my southern travels, this was one of the greatest misconceptions I heard about rescue organizations. Those I saw in operation are often investing far more in most dogs than they will ever see returned in an adoption fee.

they are there for the right reasons. If they meet the criteria, everyone should feel good about that.

"There are also some in animal control for whom euthanizing all the animals is the easy way out," she continues, suggesting some would, rather put animals down than build and manage an adoption program and establish relationships with sometimes-critical rescue organizations who may want to see changes in shelter operations. This seemed surprisingly candid for one of the officers of the state's association of animal control officers. "A lot of what we do at the Louisiana Animal Control Officers Association is basic education because so many of our members have no basic education in shelter management, infection control, and animal abuse investigation."

After lunch, Virginia walks us through the shelter. The Lafayette shelter, by contrast with Saint Martin's, is well staffed, and its budget is just under two million dollars a year. There are fifteen employees, including four animal control officers on patrol and a patrol supervisor. Five days a week, five trustees from the parish jail also work at the shelter. Lafayette Parish has about 250,000 residents, Saint Martin just 53,000.

The shelter is well lit and appears clean,

but having been in perhaps a dozen shelters by now, there's just something deeply sad about seeing dogs confined, no matter how clean and well lit the facility may be. Uniformly, the enclosures in the public shelters I saw were Spartan concrete or chain-mesh enclosures, more often than not without so much as a toy to play with or a soft place to lie down. Some, such as the Pineville shelter just outside of Alexandria, were dark and dungeonlike. Every time I walked the corridors of a shelter, the thought that always came to mind was, *These dogs don't belong here.*

As we walk by the kennels holding dogs up for direct public adoption, Virginia explains that once a dog is on "adoption row," it can stay there forever. These are the dogs Virginia thinks will be the easiest to place. Rescues, such as LAA, can have the pick of the rest, though dogs found to be aggressive will not be released, and some dogs, simply because they are breeds deemed aggressive, such as pit bulls, won't be released. There has been much debate about whether pit bulls and other so-called "bully breeds" have been unfairly stereotyped and maligned, but some communities, concerned about potential liability, simply won't take the risk of releasing some types of dogs. Sadly, one of the first dogs I see is a very sweet female pit bull whose nails are way too long, is heartworm positive, and has been overbred. She was abandoned by the side of the road when she was no longer useful for breeding.

"Every now and then, we get a special animal in," Virginia says, not referring to any specific dog. "What we do here hurts so much sometimes that if one of my employees wants to do something special for an animal, it's a way for me to help them get through the day."

With the exception of the relationship between LAA and Michelle Brignac, director of Saint Martin Parish Animal Control, and Kathy Wetmore and BARC in Houston, every shelter-rescue relationship I observed seemed marked by some degree of mutual suspicion. But shelter directors need rescues unless they are utterly indifferent to the animals in their custody, and without some degree of cooperation from the directors or staff, rescues are thwarted in their mission and lives are lost. If you're in rescue, the shelters can never be run well enough; if you're a shelter director, the rescues can be unreasonable, demanding, and mettlesome. It's a broad generalization, but it seems to capture the nature of the tension.

281

When Melinda and I return from lunch and our visit to Lafayette Animal Control, we encounter Carley Faughn, LAA's executive director, in the reception area. It's clear the relationship with Virginia is not without its tensions.

Neither Melinda nor Carley accepts the canine euthanasia number of 55 percent, though Melinda thinks it's a number Virginia believes to be true. Accurate statistics, as noted, can be hard to come by. And though they tell me Virginia and her staff are always cordial, there's an employee who works for Virginia and who they believe makes arbitrary decisions about which dogs will live and which will die. Yet they work to maintain a good working relationship in the interest of the dogs.

But we have little time to dissect the complicated shelter-rescue relationship. For Carley and the LAA staff, today is a busy day. Early tomorrow morning, as he does every other Thursday, Greg will turn up LAA's long, dirt driveway. The staff, many in tears, will say good-bye to dogs they have loved and cared for and nursed back to good health. It's bittersweet, of course. All that effort, all that love and compassion has prepared each one for a new life where they will be valued, cherished, and adored. And each one bound for a new life up north makes room for another to take his or her first steps on the same journey.

9
LONG DAY'S JOURNEY INTO NIGHT

When we last left Greg and Tommy (and me) in a tractor-trailer with more than fifty dogs at the end of Chapter 5, we were in a waterlogged parking lot east of Lafayette on I-10 on a Wednesday night. Earlier that morning we'd boarded Keri's dogs in Alexandria, then driven to Baytown and back into Louisiana. Most were settled in for a short night's sleep before we were to start boarding more dogs at Lafayette Animal Aid early the next morning. The stop at LAA will mark the beginning of the longest part of Greg's journey, a drive that begins in Lafayette early on Thursday morning and ends early Friday evening in Allentown, Pennsylvania.

Thanks to Willis and T-Bone, whose barking has kept me up most of the night, I've managed to get nary an hour of sound sleep before six thirty, when Greg and Tommy

are up and ready for the short drive to LAA. But I can't feel that bad for myself. Other than sleep, Greg doesn't get so much as five minutes off when he's on the road. Even when Tommy's driving, he's taking calls, keeping an eye on the road (he and Tommy serve as one another's second set of eyes while driving), and noodling over work-related problems, such as the need for a new trailer and how to arrange the dogs since we have a heavy load already and more to board.

Fifteen dogs are scheduled to join us at LAA. For the past few years Greg has transported between two hundred and three hundred dogs a year from LAA, all adopted out through Labs4rescue and Mutts4rescue.

Just as it did when we loaded our first dogs in Alexandria yesterday morning, it's pouring as the dogs are brought to the truck. There's Hammish, a four-year old Border collie with a leaky heart valve and advanced, inoperable heartworm disease. Though he'll likely live only another year, a Connecticut family has agreed to provide a home for whatever days he has remaining. He's a handsome dog, sweet and happy. A few of the LAA staff wipe away tears that have mingled with the raindrops on their faces as Greg picks up Hammish and lifts him into the trailer.

Following Hammish is Happy, an eight-month-old Australian shepherd mix found tied to the fence at LAA with his two brothers. Happy has really hit the lottery; he's found a forever home on Martha's Vineyard. Then Gladys and Abby, both young Lab mixes, a golden retriever named Lolly, a terrier-schnauzer mix named Maple, and last but not least, Bijou, the stray pulled from the Saint Martin Parish Animal Services shelter and bound for the Mooney family in South Walpole, Massachusetts.[27]

27. Saint Martin Parish is a neighboring parish to the east of Lafayette Parish.

Now it's time for the big thirty-six-hour push from Lafayette to Allentown. When we finish loading the dogs at LAA in the pouring rain, most of the dogs traveling with us this week are on board. We'll pick up a few more in Hammond, Louisiana — including Sadie, the Lab with epilepsy — and Slidell, Louisiana, and, near midnight, two more in tiny Rising Fawn, Georgia, in the northwest corner of the state.

Thanks to people such as Keri Toth, Greta Jones, and Sara Kelly in Alexandria; Kathy Wetmore in Houston; Melinda Falgout, Carley Faughn, April Reeves and the staff of LAA; and dozens of fosters, veterinarians, volunteers, shelter directors, and shelter staff, nearly eighty hard-luck dogs — dogs abandoned, abused, neglected, unwanted, or just lost — are about to begin the final leg of their long and often torturous journeys to their forever homes.

There's Bijou and Willis, and Tennessee, surrendered by the homeless man he'd been with for two years. There's Salyna, Sully, and Seth, three of the ten puppies saved by CJ Nash, the compassionate and quick-thinking eighteen-year-old near Natchitoches, Louisiana; Jupee and Pam, two of the tub puppies; and Trudy and her companion, Popcorn. And sadly, there are those who didn't make it or never will, nameless hundreds that looked at me through shelter cage doors, licked my fingers, and jumped manically hoping to get my attention. But for now the focus is on getting the lucky ones we have on board safely on their way to the families counting down the hours and minutes till Gotcha Day. Greg's ready to roll, the dogs are ready, and so am I.

The virtually nonstop run from Lafayette to Allentown will take us across Louisiana, through Mississippi, Alabama, a tiny piece of Georgia, Tennessee, Virginia, West Virginia, and Maryland, to Allentown, in Pennsylvania, where, if all goes according to schedule, we'll arrive around six o'clock on Friday night. It's 1,326 miles all told.

Back on Interstate 10, heading east toward Baton Rouge, it seems as if the entire state of Louisiana is sinking into the swamps. For twenty miles, the highway is straight as an arrow and elevated just feet above the Henderson Swamp, a massive wetland in Saint Martin Parish. The rain subsides near Baton Rouge, and a short distance beyond, we stop in Hammond. This is where we pick up Sadie, who will ride in the cab with us. Sadie is a sweet girl, but also self-contained. She doesn't display much emotion as we hoist her up into the cab. Rather, she sits calmly next to me on the mattress behind Greg and Tommy, tolerant of my petting her but not insistent for affection, as many dogs are, as we continue our journey east across Louisiana.

Just before noon, in a parking lot near a Cracker Barrel in Slidell, we meet volunteers from Labs4rescue and other rescue groups to load a few Labs, a basset hound, and several others.

Before we leave Slidell, Greg calls Debbie, his mother-in-law, to review the passenger list. As always, there have been some late cancellations and some substitutions. Greg wants to make sure he has an accurate list with each dog and where it's meeting its forever family or foster. Debbie will also be the point person communicating with adopters and fosters meeting the transport up north in case we're running behind schedule.

As we cross the border into Mississippi, the return of heavy rains is slowing our progress considerably and adds to the strain and fatigue we're all experiencing now. Driving in this kind of weather requires greater than usual concentration. In good weather, we've been moving at sixty to sixty-five miles per hour; now our pace has slowed to forty-five or fifty at best.

When we reach Hattiesburg, we stop briefly to deliver a load of supplies donated to a local rescue shelter from people in New England. I've come to learn this is exactly the kind of extra mile Greg travels simply because he's eager to help people — and dogs. He's not charging for hauling the food, bowls, leashes, and other pet supplies he picked up two weeks ago on his last pass through New England. He's just lending a hand to the rescue groups transporting dogs with him, and sometimes even those that aren't.

By midafternoon, crossing Mississippi, the rain abates and the roads dry out. Seeing the weariness on Greg's face on our fourth day on the road now, I ask him what keeps him going and how long he thinks he can keep doing work that is clearly exhausting, physically and mentally.

"I plan on doing this as long as I'm physically able," he tells me. "And I do it because it helps the dogs. It helps the person getting the dog, but I also do it because it helps people like April [April Reeves, the adoption coordinator at LAA]. April is one of my heroes. I want to help her too. It's why I drag my ass out of bed. As I learned with Poochie [the first stray dog he brought home as a kid], damn this feels good. And it *still* feels good."

When we stopped in Slidell, an elderly gentleman named John Yonge met the transport. He'd been fostering two Labs, Bumble and Bee, and they were now headed to their forever homes. He cried quietly as he said good-bye, just as Tilani Pomirko had when she said good-bye to Willis in Baytown, and just as Greta Jones had when she said good-bye to Tippi in Alexandria. Fosters give so much of themselves to these dogs, knowing all along there's a painful parting in the future — unless, of course, they become foster failures. Their role in the rescue process is indispensable. Without them, far fewer dogs would make it to forever homes.

"It takes a lot to scoop up a dog and give it so much of your heart knowing you're going to give it up," Greg explains. He's right: The foster networks are another piece of the rescue puzzle mostly invisible to adopters. Though he's a critical link in the rescue chain, the one knitting all the others together, you sense Greg is in this difficult, messy, smelly work for all the people who play their parts in getting the dogs on board his truck, including people like John and Tilani. "At the end of day," he says, "everyone feels good about what they've done."

On every trip, Greg stops for two to three hours outside of Birmingham, Alabama, where a group of about two-dozen volunteers meet the truck and help Greg and Tommy get every dog out for a good walk, play with them, rub their bellies, and give them water and snacks. These are the "Birmingham Angels," as Greg calls them, started a few years ago by a woman named Lynda Ingle. In 2011, Lynda, who is involved in several local rescue organizations, had rescued a dog and found an adopter in Massachusetts. Someone recommended Rescue Road Trips for transport. She started following Greg on Facebook, saw he was looking for volunteers in the area, and offered to pull a group together.

"Greg puts his all, his whole being into transporting these dogs safely," Lynda once told me. "These aren't just dogs to him."

By late afternoon, we're southeast of Birmingham on Interstate 20, on our way to meet the Angels, when we pass a white van traveling in the right lane. Greg realizes it's Keri Toth and Greta Jones from Alexandria on their way to this Sunday's adoption event in Rhode Island with forty dogs, mostly puppies. Greg expected they'd be much farther north by now, and he's concerned as evening turns to night they're going to be fatigued. He knows from experience it's no easy feat to make a long-distance drive in a van with forty mostly very young and active puppies.

We wave as we pass, and Greg calls Keri on her cell phone. He tells her she and Greta should follow him into Birmingham, that the Angels will help them with the dogs they're transporting too. Greg never expected to see Keri and Greta on the road. But this is the kind of improvisation that keeps the rescue movement moving. Knowing how difficult the trip is for Keri and Greta, Greg suggests, insists really, that we travel as a two-vehicle caravan all the way to Allentown. After all, we're carrying two-dozen "Keri dogs" bound for the Rhode Island adoption event too. Greg's going to do whatever he can to make sure all of them make it there safely and on time.

Right around 6:00 p.m., followed by Keri and Greta, we pull into the parking lot where the Angels are waiting. The skies are threatening yet again, and getting more than eighty dogs out for walks in the pouring rain would be a nightmare, not to mention the forty dogs in the van needing to get out and exercise and do their business, but we luck out and there's little more than a light drizzle as the carefully orchestrated routine unfolds.

Volunteers line up at the trailer door as Lynn Watson, dressed in jeans, a Rescue Road Trips T-shirt, a baseball cap, and rain boots ("washable and pee proof"), hops into the trailer. Lynn is one of the Angels. As each dog is taken out of its crate for a walk, she'll clean the kennel and lay down dry newspaper. Over the din of dozens of excited, barking dogs, Greg, Tommy, and Lynn hand off dogs to one another and then to the waiting volunteers.

"T-Bone!" shouts Tommy, handing T-Bone to Greg.

"T-Bone! Got him!" Greg shouts back as he slips a leash over T-Bone's head and around his neck. Then he turns to the man next in line at the trailer door.

"T-Bone!" Greg shouts as he leads T-Bone down the steps and into the hands of the waiting volunteer.

"Paper change in forty-four!" Tommy yells to Lynn, referring to T-Bone's crate number.

"Tennessee!" shouts Tommy. And the

process is repeated, with Greg, Tommy, and Lynn handing dogs to volunteers until each dog has had his time in the fresh air.

As Greg and Tommy work to get the dogs out, Keri and Greta have been setting up portable play spaces for the dogs they're driving to Rhode Island. Occasionally, a puppy slips out and a handful of volunteers chase it down. This isn't a typical stop with the Birmingham Angels; not only is Greg carrying about two-dozen dogs more than usual, but there are also the forty unexpected guests with Keri and Greta. There's more than a passing resemblance to a traveling circus. Seeing Keri and Greta have their hands full, Greg asks Lynn to lend them a hand.

"She's willing to get knee deep in shit," Greg says to me, paying her one of the highest compliments you can get from Greg Mahle.

Lynn is tall with dark, shoulder-length hair; she works in an administrative position for the University of Alabama-Birmingham Health System. There was little time to talk during our stop, so we spoke by phone a few weeks later. Greg had urged me to talk with her; she is one of his most highly prized volunteers and would be able to explain what drives the Angels to come out to meet the truck every two weeks, rain, snow, or shine.

"I always had dogs growing up," Lynn tells me, "but my father wasn't keen on it. When I was finally on my own at nineteen, my first rite of passage was to get a rescue dog. I was at an adoption event and saw this older wirehaired terrier–dachshund mix being overlooked by everyone. She wasn't one of the cute puppies in a pen. She was my companion throughout my twenties and into my thirties. We were our own pack. We traveled together. I've been drawn to rescue ever since." And to rescue dogs — she now has three.

"There's a lot of compassion out there," Lynn says, "and Facebook connected me with like-minded people helping animals one at a time." Through Facebook, Lynn learned about Lynda Ingle's group helping Greg with the dogs. When she came to meet the truck for the first time a few years ago, she was impressed.

"There wasn't a lot of 'Kumbaya,' " Lynn tells me. "Everyone was just there to help the dogs. I started helping Tommy in the truck and got hooked on the grunt work. I love being in the truck and being hands-on with all the dogs and handing them off for walks. You see the fearful ones, who are reassured when you put them into someone's arms. They know they are on the road to safety and security.

"There's always at least one that shoots an arrow right through my heart," she continues. "It's a look in the eye. It's very rewarding. Everyone can do something. Not everyone can give money or adopt or foster, but everyone can make a difference. You can't solve the whole problem, but you can have an impact. Greg knew he could make a difference and people stepped up to help."

Lynn rarely misses a Rescue Road Trip; she's someone Greg can count on seeing every other Thursday night.

"When we were done the night you came through with the truck and all those puppies in the van, I smelled so bad." She laughs. "But being with that little community for a couple of hours and helping — on the ride home, I have the best feeling ever. I'm doing my little part, but Greg is making a huge difference. I feel so content knowing Greg is back on the road; the dogs have all been walked, fed, and watered; and Greg and Tommy are okay. It's great to know they are all safe and on their way.

"I want people to realize they don't need a designer puppy from a pet shop or breeder," Lynn adds. "There are so many dogs that just don't get a chance. Caylie [her first rescue] was overlooked. She always looked like she was walking downhill because her front legs were shorter than her hind legs. But I gave her a chance and she changed my life."

Just before nine, a little less than three hours after our arrival in Birmingham, we're back on the interstate, but traffic is at a virtual standstill. Using my iPhone, I can see we have several miles like this ahead. I check the news and learn there's been a fatal accident. Under the best of circumstances, Thursday night and into Friday is the most arduous part of the journey. To be stalled right out of the gate, moving a few feet at a time, is dispiriting. It's also a reminder that this difficult job can also be dangerous. Keri and Greta manage to stay close, and for two hours, we creep along covering just three miles or so before we finally clear the accident scene and drive into the dark Alabama night, a two-vehicle caravan with five people and more than 120 dogs.

I ask Greg about the monotony of driving the same route over and over and over again. "It must seem like and endless loop," I suggest, and he agrees. When I ask him what he thinks about as the endless miles roll by he responds, enigmatically, "Everything and nothing."

I was curious what exactly this meant, so over the next twenty-four hours I would periodically and randomly ask him, "What are you thinking about right now?" The first time he was thinking about where to take Adella to celebrate their second anniversary in a few weeks, though he would be on the road on the actual date. Cincinnati was the leading contender at the moment. More often than not, he was thinking about work: from Rescue Road Trip web pages that needed updating to whether to turn the operation from a limited liability corporation to a nonprofit, to the Facebook posts he'll write as Gotcha Day draws closer. One time when I popped the question, he immediately replied, "Elvis!"

"Really?" I asked.

"Noooo!" He laughed.

Greg and Keri stay in touch by phone and about 1:30 a.m., we all pull into a rest stop in northeastern Alabama. Keri and Greta are exhausted, and it's agreed Tommy will drive the van and Keri will ride with us in the truck until we are near Knoxville. Greg's goal is to get Keri and Greta as far along as possible tonight, so they won't have such a long ride tomorrow.

With Greg behind the wheel and Keri in the passenger seat, I doze fitfully sitting on Tommy's mattress with my back against the rear of the cab, one arm around Sadie who proves to be the mellowest and sweetest of companions. The lights of small towns, larger cities (Chattanooga), and gas stations and fast food joints just off the highway seem to flicker on and off like fireflies on a warm summer evening. But mostly, all I can see are the painted lines on the highway illuminated by our headlights and the endless ribbon of highway.

Just south of Knoxville, we all stop, Keri and Tommy trade places again, and Tommy drives us on while Greg dozes for another hour or so. Keri and Greta stay put for some rest. Because we had so many dogs to be cared for in Birmingham this trip, we left about an hour later than usual. Then there was the delay caused by the accident in Birmingham. Shepherding Keri and Greta and then driving through a thick fog for the past few hours have also taken their toll. Finally, Tommy's too tired to drive any longer, and, at around 6:00 a.m., pulls into a rest area and the three of us sleep in the cab until 7:15, when Greg rouses, switches seats with Tommy, and we're rolling again.

Now, Keri and Greta are on their own . . .

sort of. The plan is now to stay in touch and rendezvous in Allentown this evening.

Normally on this drive through the night, Greg sleeps as Tommy drives and vice versa. But because he was worried about Keri and Greta, both Greg and Tommy spent several hours when both were driving. They've dealt with worse, but lots of little things have conspired to make this an especially wearying trip: the larger-than-normal load, the rain, the fog, and the accident in Birmingham. Carrying precious cargo such as rescue dogs is more stressful than transporting ordinary goods, like beer and soda. For Greg, losing valuable sleep along the way is like adding another hundred-pound weight to his shoulders.

After a fitful sleep myself, I watch the morning sun fight its way through thick fog as we cross into Virginia, Greg behind the wheel. It's around eight on Friday morning. Normally, Greg and Tommy would get each dog out for a morning walk, but the previous evening's events have put us three hours behind schedule so Greg will stop, assess each dog, and see which ones really need a walk and those that will be content to remain in their kennels. On a grassy expanse at the edge of a rest stop, Greg and I walk about three-dozen dogs as Tommy tends to the kennels.

"People think this is a glamorous job," he says to me, referring to a number of offers he's had since the *Parade* article to do a reality TV show and the minor celebrities who have asked to do a ride along. "But it's a shitty, smelly, grueling job. Who else would want to do this?" He grins. The answer is obvious: very few people, which is why my admiration for Greg grows by the mile.

A little after noon, south of Staunton, Virginia, comes a stop I've been looking forward to for four days. This is the truck stop where we'll each get a shower. For Greg, it will be the first break of any kind he's had in our five days on the road. As I saw, when he's not driving, he's taking calls, trying to sleep, thinking about the dogs, worrying about staying on schedule, cleaning kennels, or reassuring nervous dogs. Seeing him head off to the shower, change of clothes in hand, I realize this may be the only fifteen-minute break he's allowed himself since we pulled out of Zanesville.

The shower is positively rejuvenating. The exhaustion of having only six hours of sleep over three days and two nights seems to wash down the drain. All three of us are in

302

better spirits as we prepare to continue north through Virginia.

It's a good time for Greg to pull out his iPhone and painstakingly type out a new Facebook post for all those waiting down the road. Tomorrow is Gotcha Day and a steady stream of Facebook messages is part of his plan to make Gotcha Day as exciting and as memorable as it can be for everyone greeting a new dog. But this Facebook post also sums up his dedication to his work, the reason why he puts himself through these exhausting trips, driving long hours on the road through torrential rains and other bad weather, wading through and cleaning up dog poop and muck, and weathering the occasional bite or scratch to give these dogs and their soon-to-be forever families a future together.

"At this point," he writes, "the dogs and I have become a pack. We are all starting to form bonds and I have learned the personality of each of them. I am thankful for getting to share part of my life with each of them. I am happy I have such a great group of dogs to go through this experience with me. I love them all."

The ride through Virginia is the longest of any state on the route. Greg and Tommy occasionally fall into stream-of-consciousness conversation, often started by something they hear on Radio America, the conservative talk radio station Tommy listens to and that Greg largely tunes out. Maybe it's the unusually exhausting trip we've had, or the fact that they spend an inordinate amount of time in a small space together with nothing else to do, but over the course of one ten-minute period in Virginia, a conversation which begins with Tommy describing a huge moth he saw at the truck stop where we showered ricochets rapidly to the existence of Bigfoot and the Loch Ness monster to "trunk monkeys" (a reference to a series of car commercials) to aliens performing colonoscopies. They egg each other on, each trying to top the other by raising the conversation to a higher level of absurdity. The banter has a wonderful Robin Williams–esque randomness to it. It's all the more comical because of Tommy's passing resemblance to the actor John Goodman and Greg's marvelous way of laughing and talking at the same time that seems only to urge Tommy to ever higher flights of fancy.

Despite the banter, it would be a stretch to describe Greg and Tommy as friends, despite, or perhaps because of, the amount of time they spend together. Greg is indisputably in charge, and Tommy generally refers to him as "Boss." They don't see one another between trips. What Greg values is that Tommy shows up on time and does the work Greg needs him to do; it's not easy finding someone willing to do a job as demanding and dirty as this one, especially for a wage Greg can afford to pay. In truth, their relationship is as Greg needs it to be. He doesn't need a friend on the road; he needs a stalwart employee, and Tommy has never let him down in the four years or so he's been working for Greg.

"The driving can be so boring and so monotonous," Greg says to me when the latest explosion of random humor abates, apparently trying to explain the giddiness I've just witnessed. It also seems to relieve some stress. "Adhering to a schedule is my least favorite part of the job," he adds. "It would be nice to be free from that and be able to spend more time with the dogs outside. But we always have people waiting on us." He doesn't mean this as a complaint — he values every adopter for giving a dog a second chance. But when the demands of the schedule are bearing down on him, as they are today, he wishes he could give the dogs a little more of his attention.

■ ■ ■ ■

Just before 3:00 p.m., we're a few miles from the West Virginia border and we make a quick stop to check on the dogs. Sadie is still my seatmate on the mattress. We've been together like this for more than a thousand miles and she's a complete love: quiet, gentle, uncomplaining. I share my snacks with her; she rests her head in my lap.

"Adella's worried about you," Greg says to me at one point after getting off the phone with his wife. Adella knows how tough it is on the road, and she knows Greg can be sarcastic and quick-tempered, especially when he's stressed. "I told her you were fine." And, indeed, though extremely tired, I am fine, even content. It has been a long trip, and we have many miles still to travel, but the excitement of nearing the finish line and witnessing Gotcha Day is beginning to build.

Soon the South is behind us. After twenty-five miles in West Virginia and twelve in Maryland, we're in Pennsylvania, a definitively northern state.

The Maryland–Pennsylvania border is also the Mason–Dixon Line. Though it has, over time, come to unofficially demarcate the North from the South, and separated the free states from the slave states during the Civil War, the Mason–Dixon Line has its origins in a land dispute between two families, the Penns and the Calverts, dating to before the American Revolution. Charles Mason, a British astronomer, and Jeremiah Dixon, a distinguished British surveyor, completed the survey between 1763 and 1767. For Greg, the line has come to represent the moment when the dogs have safely left behind lives of neglect, abuse, and pain, and are within reach of new lives in their forever homes. On every Rescue Road Trip, he writes a Facebook post from just beyond the Mason–Dixon Line to tell people we're getting close. It's not just a historically symbolic crossing; it's a symbolic crossing for Greg, the dogs, and their forever families eagerly awaiting us.

"With yelps, howls, and wagging tails, we crossed the Mason–Dixon," he writes. "All bad memories of being homeless, starved, abused, abandoned, unwanted, and unloved were left behind us. Our thoughts are on forever families and forever love. Gotcha Day is almost here. Are you excited? Is your welcome sign ready? Get ready, we are almost there!"

A little more than two hours later, we pull into the parking lot of the Comfort Inn near Allentown, where about two-dozen Allentown Angels are waiting, another of the volunteer groups that have sprung up along Greg's route. The group formed in mid-2009 and is organized by Keith and Diane Remaly, who learned about Rescue Road Trips, as my wife and I did, when they adopted their first dog, Dallas, through Labs4rescue. The Remalys have four rescue dogs. (Dallas died shortly after this trip in June 2014, leaving the Remalys profoundly bereaved.) He's a production planner for a hydraulic equipment manufacturer; she's an engineer with Verizon.

"When my eyes got opened about what goes on down south, and how many dogs are put down, I wanted to do what I could to help," Keith told me when I was writing the *Parade* magazine piece. "It makes you want to do more for them." Through social media and word of mouth, Keith grew the Allentown Angels. Volunteers range in age from eighteen to nearly eighty. The Allentown Angels meet Greg every other Friday night, come rain or snow. One snowy winter night a volunteer plowed a large area for the dogs to walk and relieve themselves.

One dog of the thousands Keith has seen stays in his memory. "There was an American Eskimo dog I was walking, and whenever I turned to head back toward the trailer, he pulled in the other direction," Keith told me. "I knelt down and he put his paws on my legs and I talked to him. I swear as I said to him 'You're going to your new home tomorrow,' he went right back to the trailer as if he understood me."

What draws Keith and the other Angels to this parking lot every other week, even on a New Year's Eve, isn't just the dogs. It's Greg. "He's a super guy," says Keith. "His heart is as big as a Volkswagen." The Remalys even traveled to Ohio for Greg and Adella's wedding in 2012.

All along the route, I notice the intricate connections that have been made to create a network that supports and sustains all sorts of rescue efforts. When Keri has a dog she thinks needs special attention, she not only tells Greg, but she calls Keith too, so he can check on the dog when it reaches Allentown. This Friday night, she can talk to Keith in person. Even though we haven't been caravanning today, Keri and Greta pull in shortly after we do. Keith has already told his volunteers that in addition to helping Greg with the dogs in the truck, there are forty more arriving with Keri and Greta.

It's a mild, beautiful evening made even more festive by an added feature to the usual scene of dogs and people gamboling on the grass expanses adjacent to the parking lot: a potluck dinner laid out on a long table filled with salads, casseroles, and desserts. Someone even brought a gas grill and is cooking hot dogs and hamburgers. In the middle of the table is a large sheet cake with "Thank you, Rescue Road Trips" inscribed on it.

As dogs romp and play with strangers they will only know for an hour or so, one very happy couple and one very happy little dog are getting to know each another. For Willis, Gotcha Day is today: his new family, Mary Ellen and Phil Gambutti, are from nearby Easton and were waiting with their welcome sign and hearts surrendered weeks ago to a photograph of Willis they saw online. Now that he's finally in their arms, they are overcome with joy and little Willis . . . well, as always, he's just a happy little camper.

As in Birmingham, the whole scene has a carnival air, with Greg's truck the equivalent of the big top in a traveling circus. The extra attraction tonight is Keri and Greta's menagerie. Inside the trailer, two volunteers, Anita Patterson and Maureen Keenan, both wearing knee pads, jeans, gloves, and headlamps, do the job Lynn Watson does in Birmingham: they help Tommy and Greg hand off dogs and clean the kennels. They work like a well-oiled machine; they've done this task so many times, it's become a polished routine. Outside, passersby stop and watch the puppies and wonder aloud about the unusual scene they've stumbled upon.

Then, just as quickly as it began, the evening winds down. Every dog has been petted, fed, watered, and walked. As dusk turns to darkness, the food is packed away, the buffet table and grill are loaded into pickup trucks, and volunteers say their good-byes and drive away in their cars. It's suddenly and eerily quiet and empty, as if the midway at a small-town circus has been rolled up and stowed for the trip to the next town.

But just when you think this forty-hour day, a day that started yesterday morning near Lafayette, Louisiana, is over, there's yet another in a series of endless tasks to be attended to. Gotcha Day drop-offs start

311

around nine thirty tomorrow morning in New Jersey, and to ensure everything goes smoothly, Greg alphabetizes the envelopes with each dog's medical records and writes down the number of the kennel each dog is in. It may seem like a small thing, just another hour's work, but it's another in the countless tasks that never seem to end when you're on transport. And even when that's done, Greg is taking pictures of the dogs with his iPhone, pictures he can use for tomorrow's Facebook posts. At 11:00 p.m., Greg calls it a day. A very long day.

Keri and Greta are staying in the Comfort Inn parking lot for the night; we drive five minutes up the road to the parking lot of another motel where, at 5:00 a.m., Greg will meet up with P.E.T.S. (Peterson Express Transport Service), another operation, like Greg's, bringing dogs up north from southern states. Dogs bound for farther north than Connecticut will be transferred to P.E.T.S., as our Albie was, for the final leg of their journey home.

As Greg climbs into his bunk in the trailer, I settle into my sleeping bag wedged between the rows of kennels for what I hope will finally be a restful night — at least, as restful as a five-and-a-half-hour night can be. Greg ends the day as he always does, with a text to Adella, telling her he loves her. And, as he always does, he falls asleep immediately.

For the next hour or so, all is quiet, but I'm having trouble shutting my brain down. I pull out my notebook and record some of the thoughts the day's events have sparked. Yet even when exhaustion overcomes me and I tuck the notebook away in my backpack, sleep still eludes me. Then, I hear it: a dog toward the back of the trailer whimpering and starting to cry. I know it's not Willis as it was a couple of nights ago, since he's with his new forever family. I get up as quietly as I can, so as not to set off a ruckus, and discover it's Salyna, the white and yellow Lab mix with the distinctive blue tongue and dark eyes I took a fancy to when we first met in Alexandria. It was less than three days ago, but it seems like forever. After a couple of attempts to calm her, I take her from her kennel, and for the next three hours, I sit inside by the trailer door with Salyna in my arms, where she falls asleep.

Within the quiet of the trailer, I can discern the first sounds of morning, just before five, in the form of birdcalls. When I crack the trailer door to peek outside, it's still dark. I've yet to close my eyes.

10
GOTCHA DAY

Inside the trailer, the start of the new day is marked by the sound of a single dog barking, then two, and then three. Soon you can hear the sound of wagging tails brushing against kennel walls, paws scratching at kennel doors, and an occasional whimper. The sounds build gradually, as the rising din stirs more and more dogs to wakefulness, until the trailer is alive with the sounds of eighty-some dogs on the threshold of new lives.

For dozens of families waiting down the road, this is the day they've been anticipating — some for days, some for weeks, some even months. The welcome-home signs have been made, the dog beds placed before fireplaces and in cozy corners, and the balls and chew toys purchased. The life of every dog we've gotten to know these past few days will be forever changed in a few hours — and so will the lives of every family ready to welcome them home.

For Greg, this is the day that makes the endless miles of blacktop, the long absences from home, and the burden of carrying so many people's hopes and dreams on his shoulders worthwhile. Today, Trudy and Popcorn, Bijou and Piper, Baby Bella and Tennessee, Pam and Jupee, and seventy other forsaken dogs will be delivered from lives of hunger, fear, abuse, neglect, and pain. Many were days or hours or even minutes from being put down before someone stepped in and gave them a second chance at life. But for every fortunate dog stepping toward his forever home today, it's

hard not to think of all those who didn't get the lucky breaks and ended their days unloved, unwanted, and unknown in kill shelters, by the side of a road, or lost in the woods.

After transferring a handful of dogs to P.E.T.S. for the final leg of their journeys, the light of the rising sun starts to limn the eastern sky. It's a few minutes after six, and Greg eases himself behind the wheel. First he calls Keri and Greta, to make sure they're okay. We won't be traveling in tandem today; we have five stops to make, in New Jersey, New York, and Connecticut, and Keri and Greta have to get to Rhode Island to prepare for tomorrow's adoption event. Then, just before he maneuvers the stick shift into first gear, he pauses to tap out another Facebook post on his iPhone: "Your heart is pounding. You barely slept last night. Today is finally here. ITS GOT-CHA DAY!!!!!!! Feel the love! We're leaving Allentown. Pluckemin, New Jersey, now I'm all about you. I'm on time and on my way!"

A thick fog has settled into the low-lying valleys of eastern Pennsylvania this Saturday morning (Gotcha Day is always a Saturday), but as the sun climbs higher in the sky, it begins to burn off until Greg is fighting a strong solar glare; we're pointed due east, directly into the sun. He lowers the visor and grabs his sunglasses. With more than a million miles behind the wheel, Greg's driven in all kinds of conditions: high winds, snow, ice, and torrential downpours. A little solar glare is nothing more than a minor nuisance.

In little more than half an hour, we cross the Delaware River into New Jersey and the day is crisp and clear. A car passes, a horn honks, and the driver gives us a thumbs-up. Greg gets that a lot when people read the writing on the side of his rig: "Rescue Road Trips: Saving Lives Four Paws at a Time."

Knowing I won't likely have a chance after the last of the dogs has been picked up in Putnam, Connecticut — he'll be leaving almost immediately for the seven-hundred-mile drive back to Zanesville, and I'll be heading sixty miles to my home outside Boston — I ask Greg what it's like for him at the end of Gotcha Day when, suddenly, the trailer is empty and quiet. He pauses for what seems an eternity, turning the question over in his mind.

"It's a difficult emotion to explain," he finally says softly. Then, without pause, he continues. "It has opposites in it. I'm happy to be finished and excited to be going home to see Adella and Connor. But I don't like going back in the trailer because the dogs are all gone. It's lifeless and cold, plastic and metal. Right now, it's full of life in its best form. You can walk down the aisle between the rows of kennels and feel all the good stuff coming out of them. You can see it in their eyes. In Putnam, suddenly, that's all gone. It feels like a void. There was life in here just seconds ago. I'm unhappy the dogs are gone, but happy each dog has a home.

"The good part of the job, the dogs, are gone, but I feel satisfied it was a job well done," he says. "When the last dog is handed to its new family, I survey the panorama of people with their new dogs and think, *I've never seen so many happy people in one place.* The people aren't interacting with each other; they're all getting to know their dogs. They're all having the same experience. You can believe the world is a better place.

"Then they all disperse and it's just Tommy and me. Then Tommy will say, 'Boss, you or me?' and he brings me back to a different reality. His voice signals the end of my taking in the scene and reminds me the job isn't over; that it's time to drive home. When we arrive back in Mattingly's lot and park the truck, I'm usually in a good mood because we are finally done. We live with that diesel engine noise all week. The silence that follows the engine being shut off means it's over; we're home. No matter what the weather, Adella will be on the porch or in the driveway waiting for me. She tries to be the first thing I see. She makes a big effort to be there each time. The sight of her — it's what she represents: home, life, love, a comfort I can't describe. I'll hug her and not want to let go and we won't even care I'm a smelly truck driver smeared with dog shit with dirty fingernails. As soon as I step away from her, the dogs are ready to greet me. Beans and Harry first, while Treasure whines and Murphy runs in circles. They all compete for my attention. Connor will say something simple, and it's enough. The house smells like my house and I know I'm home."

All week, Greg's been using Facebook to build excitement as he drives toward Gotcha Day. It isn't because he loves using social media; rather, there's a method to his social media madness. He believes his reports from the road help strengthen the growing bonds between waiting families and their pups. He wants to do everything he can to ensure there's a happily-ever-after ending for every dog. By infusing a holiday spirit into Gotcha Day, by encouraging people to bring welcome signs, and by making something of ceremony of the handoff to each family, he believes he's helping, in a small way, to bind each family to their dog. Many are going to have their struggles as they adjust to their pup and their pup to them. If they ever waver, he hopes they'll remember Gotcha Day and why they decided to welcome a rescue dog into their lives to begin with.

"I do everything I can to set up each dog to succeed," he tells me. "The kid who gets a dog tomorrow? He won't remember me later in his life, but he will always remember his dog. And that dog is going to teach him compassion, responsibility, and to be a good person, to have goodness in his heart. I'm thinking past tomorrow, to the months and years ahead. These Facebook posts are part of trying to get the relationship between each dog and his new family off on the right foot."

At 8:00 a.m., right on schedule, we pull off of Interstate 78 in central New Jersey and head for a shopping center parking lot, our first stop of the day. About a dozen people are waiting outside their cars. This isn't one of the busier stops; most of the dogs will be getting off at the last two stops in Connecticut, at Rocky Hill and Putnam. As soon as they spot the rig, some start jumping up and down, some wave their signs, and some clap their hands. What Greg does next, he will repeat at every stop on every Gotcha Day, but even after countless Gotcha Days, it's sincere every time. The truck slows to a stop and there's a hiss as the air brakes release. Greg hops out and greets the small crowd with enthusiasm.

"Hi, everybody. I'm Greg! Are you ready?"

The response is always unanimous and enthusiastic.

Then Greg explains the procedure as Tommy swings the side doors to the trailer open. The usual cacophony rises as dozens of excited and road-weary dogs give voice to their emotions. Greg explains to the families that he will call out the names of the dog and the family there to meet them.

"When I call you, please come to the trailer doors. I will give you your paperwork and then bring your dog to you." He makes one other request, one of those little things he hopes will make the day just a little more memorable, something to help seal the forever deal. "Please, I want everyone to give a round of applause for each family as they meet their new love."

If the waiting family has a young child with them, Greg will usually hand the folder with the medical records to the child just before he brings the dog to the trailer door.

"If I give this to you," he asks one little girl, "will you be sure to take it with you when you take her to the vet?" Right away, he's conveying that with a dog comes responsibility. "Now," he says, "hold that sign up high! Be proud!" And just before he moves on to the next family, he always says to them, "Thank you. Thank you for saving a life."

About a half-dozen dogs are in the embraces of their new families within a few minutes. Some are being held, some look dazed and confused, and some are running every which way at the end of their leashes, utterly bewildered by the commotion around them. There are tears and smiles and sobs of joy everywhere you look. Children touch their dogs for the first time and get the first of many dog kisses on their faces. Straight couples, gay couples, single folks, older folks and young — there's no "traditional" forever family. All you need to create one is a heart.

When all the Pluckemin dogs are off the truck, Greg pulls out his iPhone. He tries to get a picture of every dog with its new family, pictures that will go into today's Gotcha Day Facebook album, yet another small touch that turns what could have been a simple, businesslike delivery into an occasion reminiscent of a grade-school graduation. As Greg makes the rounds taking pictures, he thanks each family again for saving a life, for making a difference. Again, in his subtle way, he wants to be sure each family feels they've done something important but understands adopting a rescue dog comes with solemn responsibilities.

About half an hour after we arrive, it's time to push on. The next stop is Nanuet, New York, about an hour away. Once again, Greg is tapping away on his iPhone just before we pull out of the parking lot. "Pluckemin, you were great!" he writes. "Nanuet, I'm all about you. I'm on time and on my way."

Just before 9:30 a.m., we pull into a commuter parking lot off Interstate 287 in Nanuet and the entire scene repeats itself: families waving signs, the handoffs, the photos, and the excitement. But off to the side, I see a middle-aged couple with a dog that didn't ride along with us, and unlike everyone else here on this beautiful morning, they're not joining in the fun. They're here to surrender their dog, Beau, a Lab-boxer mix, for transport back to Houston on Greg's next trip, back to Houston Shaggy Dog Rescue where he came from.

These owner surrenders break Greg's heart, but they're part of the job. This couple, he tells me, has fallen on hard times and can no longer afford to keep Beau. A good rescue organization will always require dogs they adopt out be returned to them if the dog has to be surrendered for any reason; they don't want their dogs turned in to shelters or over to people they haven't vetted. As the happy families with their dogs drift away into their new lives together, this couple sheepishly approaches Greg. He offers a sympathetic shoulder to the woman and assures her they're doing right by Beau. He thanks them for that. They nod silently and the moment of parting, as Greg lifts Beau into the truck and hands him to Tommy, injects a somber note into an otherwise joyous day. I wonder what Beau is making of all this: How long will it take him to understand the people he's lived with the past couple of years aren't coming back? Beau will ride back to Ohio with Greg when Gotcha Day is over. Since he'll be the only canine passenger, Greg will let him ride

325

in the cab to ease his loneliness. He'll stay at Greg's house for a week and return to Houston on Greg's next trip south.

The Park & Ride, another commuter lot just off Interstate 84 in Danbury, Connecticut, is our next stop, an hour away. Once again, Greg takes to Facebook: "Nanuet, you were great! Danbury, I'm all about you. I'm on time and on my way!"

When the now-familiar ritual ends and Greg hops back into the driver's seat, I can see from his expression something is wrong. He points to a gauge showing the air pressure in one of the brake lines dropping fast until it reaches zero. The rig isn't drivable without pressure in the lines. With about sixty dogs still on board and dozens of families waiting down the line in Rocky Hill and Putnam, we're stuck. I hold my questions; Greg's not going to be in any mood to talk about what's wrong, how long it might take to get fixed, and *how* he's going to get it fixed. He knows there's a truck stop and service area about a half hour up the highway; he calls and arranges for a mechanic to make a road service call. There's no way to know how serious the problem is, and whether it can be fixed where we are or if we're going to have to be towed in. And it means there's no way to know how long we might be delayed. Less than two hours from the end of the line and we're dead in the water. Greg knows from experience these mechanical failures are inevitable, but it doesn't make them any easier, especially when we're so close to the finish line.

We all get out of the cab. Greg paces in the parking lot, his phone to his ear. He calls Debbie, his mother-in-law. He wants her to call all the people picking up in Rocky Hill and Putnam to explain he's running late and she'll update them when she has more information. She, in turn, will ask Adella to post the news on Facebook.

I step inside the trailer to see how the dogs are doing and see that Bijou, who boarded in Lafayette, needs the paper in his kennel changed. He's about twenty pounds, built low to the ground, and surprisingly strong for his size. I lift him out and change the paper with one hand as I keep him tucked under my arm. But when I go to put him back, he resists, forces himself into my arms, and wraps his front paws over my shoulders, digging his claws into my back. I grab one of many leashes Greg keeps by the trailer door and take him for a walk up and down the parking lot where we're stranded. Then we sit on the grass and keep each other company. I give him a few belly rubs, and he lays his head in my lap. About a half hour into our wait for the mechanic, Greg, obviously stressed but trying to be courteous, wanders over and asks, "Any questions?"

I tell him my questions can wait and he seems to appreciate that I'm not pestering him about what's wrong and how long it will take to fix. My guess is he doesn't know, and asking about it isn't going to get answers or a solution any quicker.

The wait for the mechanic extends past an hour before the tow truck finally appears. I keep my distance with Bijou; I have nothing to contribute to this process.

The fix turns out to be a relatively simple one, performed on the spot, a huge relief to Greg, though we are now three hours behind schedule. He calls Debbie again to get the word out.

This was going to be one of the few trips this year when Greg was going to make a little profit, but a good chunk of it just disappeared: the repair bill comes to more than $500. But, typically for Greg, it's the least of his concerns. He has more than sixty dogs still to deliver and more than a hundred people waiting for him down the road. I don't have the heart to try and get Bijou back in his kennel, so he joins Sadie and me in the cab for the rest of the ride.

Greg makes a quick Facebook post announcing we're now ready to go, with new expected arrival times in Rocky Hill and Putnam. I text Glenna and Bill Mooney, Bijou's new family, waiting in Putnam.

"As you may know, we're running a bit late but are on the way," I write and attach a picture of Bijou taken while we were stranded in Danbury. "Bijou was upgraded to first class and is with me on the bunk in the cab. He was very eager to be out of the kennel. He is a total sweetie." Within seconds, the reply comes back: "Yea Bijou!!!!! Yippee!! Can't wait!"

We hit the road at 2:00 p.m. and arrive at Rocky Hill at 3:30, where the biggest crowd of the day is waiting. The delay has been frustrating and stressful but nothing in Greg's demeanor betrays it as he hops out of the truck and greets the crowd. He won't allow his misfortune to mar the experience for anyone else.

As in Birmingham and Allentown, there's a group of angels, volunteers who meet Greg every other week to give the dogs going on to Putnam one last walk, one last treat, and one last hug before their final destination. Among them are Sue Bradley and her husband, John, Greg's Mr. Fix-It, the man who found and retrofitted Greg's trailer, repairs broken generators, and otherwise serves as Greg's unpaid chief engineer.

Most of the Rocky Hill Angels are people who have picked up dogs from Greg, according to Annette Woodcock who helps organize the group. "We thought, *This is really neat, let's go back!*" The Rocky Hill Angels also make sure Greg and Tommy are well fed before they push on to Putnam.

Rocky Hill is where, many months earlier, the Dooley family, who were featured in the *Parade* article, picked up their black Lab puppy, Audi (since renamed Brooke), one of the pups in a litter born in a car immediately after the mama was saved just hours before she was to be euthanized. Now there are different families having the same experience the Dooleys — Liz and John, and daughters, Meagan and Lauren — had a few months ago.

Meagan and Lauren fell in love with Audi when they saw her photo on Petfinder, and less than a week later, Audi was on her way. When Greg took Audi from her crate and handed her to Meagan and Lauren that day, she was all pent-up puppy energy and licked their faces and squirmed in their arms. Tears rolled down Liz's cheeks while John stood back and grinned from ear to ear. The Dooleys had lost a beloved golden retriever two years earlier, and it took all that time until they felt ready for a new dog.

"There was such an emptiness in the house that when we finally were ready for Brooke, it was a bit overwhelming but so gratifying to hold her in our arms," she told me when I again spoke with Liz almost a year to the day after Brooke joined their family. "She's a wonderful dog," added Liz. "She's willful but so affectionate." The emotions of Brooke's Gotcha Day were still fresh. "You remember, I cried the whole time," Liz told me. "Part of it was about losing Decker, our golden retriever. When a person dies, you can't replace them. But when a dog dies, you can replace that feeling of companionship. When Brooke arrived, my kids were older and I felt like Brooke was for me and my companionship.

"I'd do it all again," said Liz. "I'd get another dog!"

Today in Rocky Hill waiting for Sadie is Brenda Byers-Britney and her daughter, Elizabeth. When they heard about the delay, they almost drove to Danbury but realized if the truck was quickly repaired, they might miss us.

When I spoke with Brenda a few months after Sadie's Gotcha Day, I learned her husband, Randy, had died of ALS (Lou Gehrig's disease) earlier in the year. They had three Labs at one point, but Randy's favorite, Rosie, had to be put to sleep due to kidney disease in the fall of 2011 — on the same day they received Randy's diagnosis. "It was the worst day of his life," Brenda told me, which would have to be an understatement. A year later another of their dogs, Molly, was also put down due to cancer.

"That left Bosco," she told me, a six-year-old chocolate Lab they'd had since he was a puppy. He missed the other dogs, but Brenda felt she couldn't take on another dog; she had to care for Randy and "knew what was coming." After Randy passed away, she knew she wanted another dog.

"I went to Petfinder and was looking for a five-, six-, or seven-year-old female. I looked at only two dogs and saw Sadie had epilepsy," Brenda told me. "Rosie also had epilepsy, though no one knew at the time we adopted her." Rosie, like Sadie, was adopted through Labs4rescue. "I knew people would be scared off — the seizures can be scary — and that's why I picked her. I knew she was meant for me."

When I later asked Brenda about her emotions the day she picked up Sadie, the tears flowed, just as they had on Gotcha Day. "I was crying the entire time. I was so happy to be getting her." As gently as I could, I asked her if her tears might also have had something to do with Randy.

"Randy told me to be sure and get another dog because I had so much love to give," she replied, her voice quavering.

Her daughter Elizabeth recalls being nervous more than anything. "I was nervous because we'd gotten dogs before that didn't get along with our other dogs at first. I was worried Sadie might not get along with Bosco." Bosco, it turns out, was more unsure of Sadie than Sadie was of him, but they now get along handsomely.

As we prepare to leave Rocky Hill for the final stop, I feel a twinge of sadness. I've grown very attached to Salyna, and in Putnam, a volunteer foster is going to pick her up for the night and bring her to the adoption event in Warwick, Rhode Island, tomorrow. We have about twenty dogs bound for the event, dogs that will join the forty Keri and Greta have been driving up. My wife, Judy, and I have been talking about adopting a second dog to join Albie for some time now, but neither of us feels prepared to raise a puppy at this stage in our lives. At twelve weeks, Salyna is all puppy. I'm going to miss her.

The afternoon wears on, and it's almost early evening by the time we reach Putnam in northeastern Connecticut, the final stop on each of Greg's rescue road trips. The largest crowd of the day is waiting here; between the dogs being picked up by volunteers for the adoption event and dogs meeting their forever families, there are about fifty people, including Judy who has brought Albie along. I wonder: *Will Albie remember Greg? Will he remember this truck that brought him north from Louisiana two years ago?*

As we pull into the parking lot of an auto parts store just off Interstate 395, people break into cheers and applause and the welcome signs start waving. It's a scene Greg has witnessed countless times, but it never gets old. In a moment, he'll leap from the cab and greet the crowd as he always does. He's weary, unshaven, and unkempt from long, hard days on the road, but he suddenly turns philosophical. He surveys the scene before him from the cab, sighs deeply and turns to me.

"You know, a few days ago, these dogs

were all going to die," he says. "Now the doors will open, the light will pour in, and each one will be delivered into the arms of a loving family. *This* is heaven."

As Greg and Tommy hand dogs to the fosters and the forever families, I put my arms around my wife and then give Albie a huge hug. If he recognizes the truck or Greg, he doesn't show it. His focus is just on us, his forever family, now.

But making this trip has helped me understand where he came from, the long odds he and so many others like him face to survive, and how a series of strangers extended themselves to him and helped him make his way to us, including Greg.

The lows in rescue, I realize, are matched by the incredible highs, and without one, there isn't the other. I've met so many selfless, good-hearted people from all walks of life and different parts of the country, all connected by their love of dogs and willingness to go the extra mile — or a few thousand — to shepherd them along on their arduous journeys to love and safety. As Greg told me, everyone has a part to play, and every job in rescue is essential to the process. Some risk life and limb, some their financial security, but all risk losing and regaining pieces of their hearts over and over again.

When Anne Garnett, the volunteer foster who will be taking Salyna home for the night identifies herself to Greg, I introduce myself to her. I was under the impression from Keri she was likely to adopt Salyna herself and I'm surprised when she tells me that's not the case, that she's definitely bringing her to the adoption event tomorrow. I'd been planning all along to go to Rhode Island to see the dozens of dogs I've been traveling with the past few days find their new families, so I know I'll see Salyna one last time. Even so, as Anne drives off with her in the backseat of her car, my heart drops. Where will she go? Who will adopt her? Will they be good to this little, white-and-yellow dog with the blue tongue I met a few days, and more than a thousand miles, ago, the one I held in my arms for three hours last night as she slept?

Greg lingers for an hour or so, taking pictures and chatting with families who will join the thousands of others who already believe he's an angel or a hero, or both. It's been a very tiring day, and Greg and Tommy have hundreds of miles to go before they sleep tonight — somewhere by the side of the road in central Pennsylvania.

Greg climbs back behind the wheel and sends one final dispatch to Facebook. It's the way he signs off at the end of every Gotcha Day: "Thanks for following this week's journey. It was great having you along on the ride. I'm 700 miles from a hot shower, a real bed to sleep in, and loved ones that miss me. See you on my next Rescue Road Trip. My name is Greg . . . I help Save Lives!!"

EPILOGUE

A few months after my travels with Greg ended, I checked in with a few of the families we'd met on Gotcha Day and, in some cases, visited them and their dogs. I wanted to follow up to see what had become of some of the other dogs I'd met while on the road with Greg. Their journeys didn't really end when Greg delivered them into the arms of their new families; in some ways, they were beginning anew.

"Willis is loved by everyone he meets," Phil Gambutti told me by phone from his home in Pennsylvania. "Everyone comments on how happy and friendly he is. He knows we are his family." Poor vision doesn't seem to hinder this little marching drummer boy in any way.

"He likes to sleep right on my pillow," Phil said, "but he's small and needs help getting up on the bed. When I try to help him up,

he runs away and makes a game of it."

The Gambuttis are in regular touch with Tilani Pomerko, the young vet tech who fostered Willis for a year and who was heart-broken about saying good-bye to him. They've even invited Tilani to visit them and Willis in Florida, where they live for part of the year.

"We have no regrets at all," said Phil. "I am so glad Mary Ellen found Willis and that we could get him up here. He's such a good friend."

■ ■ ■

When I called Glenna Mooney in South
Walpole, Massachusetts, about Bijou, pulled
by LAA from the Saint Martin Parish
shelter, he sounded just like the little
powerhouse who clung fiercely to me when
I cleaned his kennel in Danbury and rode
in my lap all the way to Putnam.

"When we got in the car on Gotcha Day,
the ride home was tough because he just
pressed against me the whole time," she told
me. "He's only twenty pounds, but he's a
forty pounder when he wants to snuggle,
and he's a cuddle dog at every opportunity."
Bijou and his canine big brother, Rico, a
rescue from Puerto Rico, became fast
friends, partly because Rico was grieving
the loss of the Mooneys' other dog, Loki.
An American Eskimo dog the Mooneys
raised since puppyhood, Loki was fourteen
when he passed and had been Rico's companion since Rico arrived at the Mooneys'
several years ago. He was depressed and
lethargic, and would go outside only to do
his business. But once Bijou arrived, about
six weeks after Loki died, he regained his
energy and started eating more. "Rico licks
Bijou's face every night at bedtime," Glenna

told me. "He's so attachable and adorable."

About a week later, I went to visit Bijou to see for myself how he had settled in. Rico doesn't just lick Bijou's face at bedtime; he plants his dog kisses on him *all* the time. Bijou was a bit shy around me; he didn't appear to remember me, but was obviously very attached to Glenna and Bill, often putting his paws on their laps and staring at their faces. The transition has been a smooth one, and the Mooneys are as smitten with Bijou as he is with them.

I spoke to Brenda Byers-Britney a few months after Sadie joined her, and she told me she and her daughter, Elizabeth, had been the first ones to arrive at the parking lot in Rocky Hill on their Gotcha Day. Brenda and Sadie's original family, the one who had to surrender her because their son developed severe allergies, communicated beforehand, and the two families remain in touch on Facebook.

Sadie had no seizures the first two and a half months she was with Brenda, but in mid-August suffered three within a half hour. Brenda rushed her to the vet, where she stayed overnight. She was concerned perhaps something else was wrong, but an MRI showed no other problems. For a week she was fine, then had another seizure in the bed she shares with Brenda and then several more.

"She loves chewing on knucklebones — she can do it for hours — but I noticed they caused her to poop more often and wondered if she was passing her medication too quickly," Brenda told me. Her vet said it was possible but seemed skeptical. Brenda discontinued the knucklebones and Sadie has been seizure free since.

Bosco, Brenda's 120-pound chocolate Lab, and sixty-pound Sadie run and play together. "She's a crazy dog," Brenda told me. "I've always had Labs, and she's the fastest runner I've ever seen." Sadie was so mellow and sedate when I rode with her on transport, it was hard to imagine she's so active, but like many rescue dogs, her personality revealed itself over time.

"It took a little while, a week or so, for her to feel at home, but every day it got better," Elizabeth told me. "My mom is the caretaker; they're her babies."

The Frampton family of Cumberland, Rhode Island, adopted Trudy and Popcorn (now Rudy), her companion, at the Rhode Island adoption event.

"It was divine intervention," Elizabeth

Frampton told me several months later. The Frampton's fifteen-year-old son, J. W., was born blind. Ten surgeries by age two restored some of his sight, but he remains legally blind. They also have two daughters, ages twelve and thirteen. "I don't feel any bias about disabilities," Elizabeth told me. "I was an advocate for ten years for the rights of blind children in the state educational system. And I'm very comfortable with animals. We already had two rescue dogs when we adopted Trudy and Rudy."

They didn't have to adopt both, but seeing how attached they were, they didn't want to separate them. "Rudy really is Trudy's guide dog," Elizabeth adds. "They run up and down — we have a large piece of property — but if Trudy wanders too far for her comfort or mine, I tell Rudy to get her and he does."

Still, it's been a huge undertaking. Early on, the Framptons thought they might have to re-home Trudy and Rudy. There were other major stressors in their lives at the time, but they ultimately concluded they'd made a commitment and it would be unfair to the dogs to move them again. "It's a work in progress," says Elizabeth, "but we're making progress."

■ ■ ■ ■

A few months after he'd been adopted at the Rhode Island adoption event, I drove to Cranston, Rhode Island, for a reunion with T-Bone, who conspired with Willis to keep me up most of our third night on the road. His new family is Diana Ducharme, an attorney, and her children, Luke and Tara McInerney, fifteen and eleven. A third daughter, Lauren, is attending college in Maryland.

Two years ago, the Ducharmes adopted Penny, a little terrier mix, from West Virginia. T-Bone, now Bo, is their second rescue dog. "We were committed to rescue dogs," Diana told me. "There are so many discarded animals. It's the right thing to do."

Penny is a fluffy little dog, and Luke wanted "a big boy's dog," as Diana described it, but she insisted they get an adult dog, one that was housetrained and would be a calming influence. Penny is a handful. Tara didn't want another dog; she was concerned Penny would be jealous, and since Penny required a lot of attention, she wondered how they were going to take care of another dog.

But Luke prevailed and when they went to the adoption event it was late, 3:30 p.m., but there were still over a hundred dogs available from various rescue groups. When they saw Bo, he was lying calmly on the floor.

"He seemed to have a good character," Diana told me, "and he was calm. I explained we needed a quiet dog, and the people we spoke to said he was very quiet."

Five days later, Diana realized he had probably just been exhausted because Bo has a lot of energy and hasn't been the calming influence she had hope for. It took some time for Penny to adjust, and Bo showed some aggression when Penny got near his food, so they have to feed them in different rooms. Bo is still a bit rambunctious — he jumps on people and has torn four of his dog beds apart — but very affectionate. They love him and are committed to working with him to improve his behavior.

As for Tennessee, the yellow Lab mix surrendered by a homeless man in Louisiana, his new family, the Doyles,[28] renamed him Walter. "It's been smooth overall," Jim

28. The family requested I use a pseudonym.

Doyle told me.

The Doyles had previously adopted two other rescue dogs, one, like Walter, came through Labs4rescue. "There's no need to purchase a dog when there are so many rescue dogs available," Jim told me. "Getting a rescue was a no-brainer, and going to a breeder wasn't an option." The Doyle children, a nine-year-old girl and an eleven-year-old boy, are actively engaged in Walter's care; they walk him, feed him, and give him water. They've grown up with dogs all their lives — the Doyle's oldest rescue dog has been with the family since he was a puppy and is now fourteen.

"He had a few accidents in the house," Jim told me. "I'm not sure if it's because he wasn't used to living in a house, but he's not a chewer and he doesn't get up on the furniture. One challenge is that he jumps up on people for attention and we're working on that."

Not all of the stories had happy endings, of course. Alicia McCarty of the Forgotten Dogs of the Fifth Ward Project in Houston sent an update on the boxer mix pair, since named Gavin and Gwen, we found living under an abandoned house the evening we spent together. "She only had three babies survive the litter she had a couple months ago, and people have stolen all of them," she wrote. "I hadn't seen the male the last two times I was out there and was worried sick. When we got there last night, my worst fear had become a reality. The male was injured pretty badly, and it was obvious he had been hit by a car. We are afraid he might lose the leg but won't know until we can get him to the vet."

Gavin survived but will have lifelong health issues and is with a permanent foster. Gwen found a forever home in Houston.

Alicia also wrote about Kaiser, the old dog she wanted to help die in comfort. A week after my visit, Kaiser's owners allowed Alicia to take Kaiser home with her for whatever time he had remaining. Alicia and other fosters cared for Kaiser until he died on November 22, 2014, having spent nearly his entire life on the street.

I also received news from Keri Toth about some of the dogs we'd seen the day we visited the two open-air pens that serve as the animal control facility in Colfax, Louisiana. There were three black Lab puppies there that day; all died within days of parvo. A small terrier, the sister of the dead dog Keri spotted in the doghouse, also had parvo but survived and, as of this writing, is being fostered by Greta, as is Handrietta, the dog she was sure was sister to Handley, one of her dogs. Others also survived and, again, as of this writing, are listed for adoption with Labs4rescue or Mutts4rescue.

But there was distressing news about the pregnant basset hound–rat terrier mix, the one Keri and Greta were going to buy cedar chips for so she'd have a soft place to deliver her pups.

"All of her puppies died within ten days," Keri wrote to me. "We found the last one had crawled through the chain link and made it partially down the hill in the woods behind those kennels. Its eyes weren't even open. [Some] . . . were killed by the other dogs in the kennels, since there is no real separation. [We] went to the kennels and found [the mama] crying and whimpering and digging at the fence on the concrete. We helped her jail break by using all of our might and pulling the fence up slightly and letting her squeeze through. The next thing is heartbreaking. She ran down the hill, picked up her deceased baby in her mouth, brought it to us, and started cleaning him as if he were alive. We picked him up; she jumped up to take him back; the whole time she was crying. She got him back and lay

349

down, curled up, and tried to nurse him. So I took her home with me. Her name is [now] Tillie."

Tillie found her forever home in Marston Mills, Massachusetts, a few months later, and Keri reports that she is "doing awesome in her new home up there . . . loving life."

And what became of Teddy, the poor, fearful shepherd mix we tried to board in Alexandria, the one that nipped both Greg and Mr. Robin in the hands? Teddy stayed at the Haas Animal Hospital for a while as Keri tried to help him overcome his fear and get him ready for adoption.

"For two months . . . he adored me and I adored him," Keri texted me many months later. When she thought he was ready for a new home, she brought him to an adoption event where he got spooked and bit Keri in the upper arm, delivering a serious bruise.

"I couldn't bring myself to euthanize him," Keri wrote, "and he showed he was very sorry afterward." But after some other close calls where he tried to bite people, Keri realized it would be dangerous to try and place him in an adoptive home.

"I decided to euthanize him," Keri wrote. "I sat on the floor crying, telling him how sorry I was. I am so sorry, Teddy. He was wiggling and trying to find out why I was sad. He was kissing all the tears off my face and nibbling on my hair. I loved him so. I was [angry] at the people who dumped their irresponsibility onto us. Angry that they weren't feeling the pain and heartbreak. I was second-guessing myself, as was the staff. [Dr. Haas] loved him too. He was kissing her face, sitting like a gentleman, so I wanted to try him again [and] bring him home.

"Then someone came into the clinic," Keri continued, "and Doc [referring to Dr. Haas] was sitting [in the waiting room] telling them what was going on. I brought Teddy up. He put his head in Doc's lap. She stroked him and he kissed me. Then I saw a sudden change in his eye, a look of instant confusion." Keri wrote it was a good thing she had a good grip on his collar because Teddy suddenly and with great force lunged at Dr. Haas's face, growling, and snapped, missing her face by less than in inch.

"He sealed his fate," Keri wrote. "It was still very hard as we put him on the table. He kissed all of us, all the employees, and wagged his tail until he slowly went to sleep.

"I went outside and cried and dry heaved, a gut-wrenching cry, true weeping. Angry that I had to make that decision. I am so sorry, Peter, it's not a fairy-tale ending. I tried for months. I tried. I loved him like no one ever did."

Last, but not least, of course, there is Salyna. For her, there was a very happily-ever-after ending.

Early on the morning after Gotcha Day, following a fitful night's sleep, Judy and I drove to Warwick, Rhode Island, about an hour's trip, for the adoption event where twenty of the dogs we'd transported, and the forty Keri and Greta had driven in the van, would be up for adoption. I had no idea what these events were like and was surprised to see hundreds of cars and long lines of people waiting for the doors to open at 9:00 a.m.

Organized by a group called Always Adopt, and held at Balise Toyota Scion of Warwick, a large car dealership, more than a dozen rescue groups were represented. A volunteer handed out little maps showing where each rescue group was set up in the massive service bay. Most of those here had already completed adoption applications — though not for a specific dog — and been preapproved, they weren't just people who happened by and were picking up a dog on a whim, though some were.

I'd thought about Salyna all night, as had Judy. We were torn. Our youngest child was now in college. We were empty nesters. Did we really want all the work that goes with raising a puppy? Did we want to be tethered to home just at the point in our lives when we had more freedom? How would Albie adjust to a puppy? But we were both smitten. Our hearts were saying yes; our heads, no.

As I waited in line, Judy went inside to use the restroom, where she discovered she could just wander into the meticulously clean service area where the rescue groups were preparing to greet the hoards waiting outside. She called me from the entrance and waved for me to follow. Once inside, we headed straight to where Keri, Greta, and Bethany Hickey, the major domo of Mutts4rescue, were set up with sixty dogs, all now familiar to me from our days on the road together. I scooped Salyna up and held her in my arms, just as I had for many hours over the past several days.

Judy and I were flummoxed. We didn't know what to do. Salyna was an unusually beautiful puppy — even in a sea of adorable puppies — and mellow too. Her black nose and dark eyes — she looked like she was wearing black eyeliner — stood out starkly from her yellowish white fur. Within minutes of the doors' opening, half a dozen people rushed up and asked, "Are you adopting her? If not, I will."

None of these people knew anything about her, not even where she'd come from. I'd ridden with her all the way from Alexandria, Louisiana, where she'd boarded the transport in the pouring rain. I'd held her in my lap on the drive to Baytown, Texas, and walked her in the heat of the afternoon in Cajun country. For three sleepless nights in the trailer, I had visited her kennel, given her little treats, changed the newspaper when it was wet or soiled, and let her lick my fingers. On the third night, she had curled up in my arms for hours until the faint sound of chirping birds signaled the arrival of Gotcha Day. Even though we hadn't filled out an application, because we had previously adopted through Labs4rescue, Keri told us, we were pre-approved to adopt at this event.

Apparently those were the magic words we needed to hear. We didn't change her name, just the spelling, to Salina. Right from the start, she and Albie would go off leash on our walks in the woods. She followed him everywhere and could be trusted not to run away. She and Albie play, occasionally growl at each other, and compete for attention. She's an instigator, and even when she weighed a quarter of what he weighs, she would give as good as she got. On car trips, he allows her to rest her head on his back and sometimes falls asleep sitting up because she's taking up the entire backseat.

But the first couple of weeks weren't easy. We felt like prisoners in our own house and immediately had second thoughts. We had pee and poop to clean up. We were overwhelmed by both the advice books and by the responsibility of caring for two rescue dogs now. We lost sleep wondering if we'd done the right thing. (It should also be noted, we had disregarded the advice I'm about to offer in the Author's Note about not being impulsive when deciding to adopt a dog. So do as I say, not as I do in this case!)

Within a week, however, Salyna-now-Salina was house-trained, with only a few minor mishaps thereafter. We found we were able to leave Albie and Salina at home for a few hours and return to an intact house. More quickly than we imagined, life returned to normal and Salina became, as Albie had before her, part of our family.

It was because we adopted Salina that on my return trip to Louisiana — to spend time walking the shelters, visiting Dumpster sites with Keri and Greta, and meeting up again with Greg — that I drove to Natchitoches to meet CJ Nash and his family and to see where Salina was born to CJ's dog, Mia. Salina and her littermates were fortunate to have CJ as their protector. Countless litters like theirs are abandoned or brought to rural shelters where their lives are measured in hours.

About a month after we brought Salina home, I was walking her by the local garage where we get our cars repaired. Scotty, one of the mechanics, loves dogs and always enjoys seeing Albie. When he saw me with Salina, he came out to meet her. I told him she had recently come from Louisiana.

"That's funny," he said. "My brother just adopted a black Lab that came up from Louisiana too. Some guy brought him up in this truck, where people go with signs and meet their dogs. The dog's name is Hunter, but I think his name was Seth. He changed it."

Scotty's brother, Dylan, lives about a mile from us. I was sure Hunter had to be the Seth, one of the S puppies, who traveled north with us. The timing of his arrival, the name, the description of the transport — it all fit. I texted Keri to see if Seth had gone to an adopter named Dylan in Dedham, Massachusetts.[29] He had, and within an hour, Salina and I were back at the gas station with Dylan and Hunter. It was clear the puppies remembered one another. Dylan told me Hunter was never submissive with other dogs, yet he rolled onto his back and let Salina jump all over him without protest.

In time, with the help of Rae McManus, the woman CJ Nash called to help him save the puppies, and Keri, I had connected with five of the adopting families of Salina's litter; one of them was the Remalys, the couple that organizes the Allentown Angels. They adopted Sam, now Beau, who made the trip with Keri and Greta in the van, but who became ill and needed to travel back to Louisiana before being put up for adoption.

Now, Salina is an integral part of our lives. She's a composed and self-possessed young dog, wily, playful, and still as pretty as she was when she was just a little puppy. We

29. Hunter, it turned out, was one of the dogs Greg transferred to P.E.T.S. in Allentown since Dylan was picking him up in Massachusetts. That's why we didn't meet on Gotcha Day.

love her. Just as importantly, Albie loves her
too.

AUTHOR'S NOTE

In the course of writing this book, I made three trips with Greg Mahle, including one complete trip from his Ohio home to the last drop-off point in Connecticut. To simplify the narrative, I took the liberty of presenting my travels with Greg as single trip, except where I explicitly note otherwise. There were also times when I spoke to people interviewed for this book several times, sometimes in person and sometimes by phone, but again, for clarity of presentation, I have at times presented those conversations as having occurred on one occasion. In no case has this poetic license compromised the accuracy or veracity of the narrative.

This book is the story of one transporter, Greg Mahle, and three rescue organizations that account for the vast majority of dogs he transports each year, just one small network of people working to save the lives of southern dogs.[30]

But the world of rescue is far larger than Greg and the organizations he works with. There are many other excellent rescue organizations and transporters out there. There are also many you should avoid.

30. A few months after my travels with Greg ended, I learned he was no longer transporting dogs for Lafayette Animal Aid. As in any human endeavor, there are politics in rescue too, and differences of opinion about how things should be done. Greg describes their parting as a difference in philosophy regarding adoptions. I think very highly of both Greg and LAA. Both have the best interests of the dogs very much at heart. April Reeves, who had served as LAA's adoption coordinator for ten years, has since left the organization, though she continues to work with both Labs4rescue and Mutts4rescue. Jamie Clark, the volunteer I met at the shelter in Saint Martin Parish, now has April's former position. Keri and her organization are also now doing more of their own transport using a van, so Greg no longer stops in Alexandria either. He still stops in Lafayette, so Keri brings any dogs she's sending with Greg to Lafayette, where she brought Albie. Greg's route now takes him farther west into Texas and includes Austin, Columbus, (an hour east of San Antonio) and Katy, a bit west of Houston.

Those happy scenes when Greg pulls his truck into the parking lots on Gotcha Day are wonderful, but as Anne Lindsay, president of the Massachusetts Animal Coalition told me, "There aren't always happy endings for rescue dogs." Too often those unhappy endings result because people underestimated the time and effort required to make a successful life with a dog, or simply have little understanding of a dog's world. Sometimes they've adopted through a rescue organization that doesn't thoroughly evaluate their dogs to maximize the chances of a successful placement.

People fall in love with pictures of dogs online or at first sight at adoption events. But life for that adorable dog will become dull, frustrating, and perhaps even dangerous for the dog and people if you aren't fully committed and don't try to understand the world as your dog experiences it. Alexandra Horowitz's book *Inside of a Dog: What Dogs See, Smell, and Know* should be required reading for anyone adopting a rescue dog or buying a dog from a breeder. Her book is not a training manual, but it will almost certainly inform your relationship with your dog for the better. Above all, your dog needs and deserves your empathy.

As anyone who has truly loved a dog will

tell you, there are countless moments of great tenderness, joy, and transcendent happiness. But as in any relationship, it's not always butterflies and a joyous romp through fields of waving grain. It can be very hard work; it will try your patience repeatedly, and there are no guarantees with any dog.

Before you make the commitment, you need to be brutally honest with yourself. Do you have the time, and will you have the energy — now and twelve to fourteen years from now — to meet your dog's needs for exercise, companionship, happiness, and healthy growth? Do you have the patience to let your dog be a dog? If you're adopting a puppy, that adorable little bundle of fur you just want to cuddle is going to shred your favorite scarf and destroy your best pair of dress shoes. She's going to poop on your handmade Persian rug. She's going to grow up and become an adult dog, maybe a little less cuddly and adorable than she was as a puppy, just as babies become rebellious teenagers and young adults. If you adopt a younger dog — a year or two past puppyhood, such as Albie — even his personality will evolve over time. The docile, grateful stray who seems so eager to please the first year may become more assertive as he or she becomes more accustomed to being in your home and with your family. You need to understand that as with children, certain personality traits may be fixed, but others change over time. You need to go with the flow.

There are, to be sure, dogs who are too aggressive or who are unable to trust people for reasons not of their own making. There are legitimate reasons why people sometimes have to part ways with a dog. But far too often dogs are victims of unrealistic expectations.

Your job isn't to train the dog to live like a person, but to train yourself to live with a dog. Just as with kids, you need to be in control and not let the inmates run the asylum, but the more you expect your dog to behave like a person, the more frustrated you will be and the more unhappy the dog will be. You may want to take a brisk walk when all your dog wants to do is stop every three feet and explore his fantastic and lavish world of smell. You may want to sleep in on a bitter February morning when every paved surface is covered in ice and snow, but your dog still needs to get out and do her business. And trust me, your dog has no interest in NFL Football or *American Idol* and doesn't understand your elaborate oratory. It's remarkable how many people get angry at their dogs because they haven't grasped the fact that while dogs will learn to respond to certain commands, they do not have a command of the English language.

Having considered all of the demands and responsibilities having a dog will entail, if you decide to adopt a rescue dog, the first step you can take to make your own rescue journey successful is to work with a reputable rescue organization.

Such groups are serious about trying to ensure successful adoptions. Just as there are good doctors and bad; honest, reliable contractors and dishonest, unreliable ones; the same applies to the bewildering, fractious, and often contentious world of canine rescue. Some calling themselves "rescue" organizations are simply an individual or two out to make a few bucks, scooping up stray dogs — healthy or not — in, say, Tennessee, driving them north, and selling them on street corners. That's not a rescue organization; it's a disaster. And as I saw and heard often while writing this book, canine rescue work attracts its fair share of what many, even in rescue, call "crazies" — people who deeply believe they are saving dogs but who operate irresponsibly, often heedless of any standards. Their antics often tar the entire rescue community and make life more difficult for those who are working tirelessly to assure healthy, happy lives for hard-luck dogs.

If you were hiring a lawyer, looking for a doctor, or engaging a contractor, you'd ask for recommendations from people you trust. You should do the same when you decide to adopt a rescue dog. Ask around. Have people had a good experience with the rescue organization in question? Ask veterinarians too. Have they heard of the group you are thinking of adopting through? If so, what do they know? Can they recommend a group with a solid history and reputation?

Second, your rescue dog should be fully up-to-date on all vaccines and should be spayed or neutered. Once you know the age of the dog you are interested in adopting, ask a vet what vaccines the dog should already have had. Your dog may need additional vaccines upon arrival, but should be current at the time of transport or, if in a local foster home, at the time of adoption. Ask your rescue organization if that's the case, and when in doubt, ask to see the medical records. No one can absolutely guarantee a dog's health — they can contract illnesses during transport, or test heartworm negative but turn out to have the disease, but you can minimize the risks by asking questions and making sure the dog has been treated for any existing conditions and been vaccinated to prevent others.

A sign that you're working with a reputable rescue is the home visit. Before Labs4rescue will allow you to adopt one of their dogs, for example, a volunteer will come to your home, meet your family, ask a series of questions, and evaluate the home environment. The volunteer may arrive with his or her own dog in tow to see how you relate to dogs. If you have other pets, some, such as Houston Shaggy Dog Rescue, will call your veterinarian to see if you are meeting all of the animal's health needs. While you're checking the dog out online, they're checking you out. Yes, all rescues are interested in moving dogs into homes expeditiously because each one adopted out opens up an opportunity to save another life, but not at the risk of settling a dog into a home where the chances of success aren't high. Their responsibility also extends indefinitely: if for any reason you need to surrender the dog, most reputable rescue organizations require in the adoption contract that you surrender the dog to them.

They don't want you passing the dog off to someone they haven't vetted or, worse still, to a shelter where the dog may be euthanized.

While no one can guarantee a dog perfect in health and temperament, adopting a rescue dog needn't be a pig in a poke either, and tens of thousands of people can attest to the wonderfulness of rescue dogs they've saved from near certain oblivion in Louisiana, Texas, Mississippi or, in smaller numbers, states north of the Mason–Dixon Line. And when a rescue dog finds a loving forever home, it's a happy ending and a new beginning for dog and family alike.

When I walk Albie and people ask about him — how old is he, is he a purebred Lab, where did he come from — I always say he's a rescue from Louisiana and about four or five years old; we don't know for sure. Often the next question is, "Is he a Katrina dog?" Hurricane Katrina hit Louisiana in 2005 and Albie is, as of this writing, only five years old at most. He was born well after Katrina. It's important to understand the overpopulation of southern dogs is not the result of a single event; it's an ongoing, chronic problem and it's been ongoing since well before Katrina.

One of the thoughts that plagued me while I was growing attached to Salina and starting to think about adopting her is that puppies are the most adoptable of all rescue dogs. Once they are in the safety of a rescue organization, they aren't hard to place. Dogs like Albie, who was two or three years old when we adopted him, are also relatively easy to place. Special needs dogs such as Sadie, the yellow Lab with epilepsy, and senior dogs, those in the last half of their expected life-span, are harder to place: they will be more illness prone in their later years and people are reluctant, understandably, to give their hearts to a dog who may live only another few years. Yet there are many wonderful older dogs and dogs with special needs, and you see their profiles on Petfinder month after month after month. It takes a special person to commit to a senior dog or one with special needs. As Greg watched me grow increasingly infatuated with Salina, he reminded me of that and I took it seriously. I knew we would be doing an older dog a greater service than we would Salina by adopting her; she would have no trouble finding a forever home. But by the time we had reached New England, we were connected and I couldn't bear to abruptly break that bond. She'd have moved on easily had we not adopted her. I'm not so sure I would have. As is probably clear by now, rescue is a matter of the heart, but use your head too!

YOU CAN HELP! SUPPORT THE RESCUE ORGANIZATIONS IN THIS BOOK

Please consider supporting the work of some of the rescue organizations mentioned in this book. Most of those listed below have links on their websites if you wish to donate online.

Rescue Road Trips
P.O. Box 107
White Cottage, OH 43791
www.rescueroadtrips.com/Rescue_Road
  _Trips.html

CenLa Alliance for Animals
P.O. Box 8641
Alexandria, LA 1306-1641
www.cenlaanimals.com

Companion Animal Outreach
P.O. Box 1415
Kemah, TX 77565

Forgotten Dogs of the Fifth Ward Project
P.O. Box 506
Porter, TX 77365
www.forgottendogs.org

Houston Shaggy Dog Rescue
kathy@houstonshaggydogrescue.org
www.houstonshaggydogrescue.org

Labs4rescue
P.O. Box 955
Killingworth, CT 06419
www.labs4rescue.com

Lafayette Animal Aid
P.O. Box 298
Carencro, LA 70520
www.lafayetteanimalaid.org

Mutts4rescue
www.mutts4rescue.org

To support Tom English's work at the Brazoria, Texas County Shelter, please donate to 31Paws; that organization helps fund the medical supplies Tom needs to help the Brazoria dogs. You may specify that you want your donation to go to Brazoria:

31Paws
P.O. Box 8255
Bend, OR 97708
www.31paws.org

ACKNOWLEDGMENTS

It takes a village to create a book, just as it takes a village to rescue a dog, and attempting to recognize and thank everyone who lent a hand along the way is rife with the risk that you will forget someone. To anyone I inadvertently overlook, my apologies.

First and foremost, of course, I am deeply indebted to Greg Mahle and his wonderful wife, Adella. Greg brought our Albie to us from Louisiana and for that alone, I am deeply in his debt. Greg is, at his core, a private person, and his rig is his home away from home when he's on the road. It's a tiny, self-contained little world, and until I hopped aboard, no one had ever been invited to ride along. It was a great privilege to share this private world with him. And obviously, without Greg, this book would not and could not exist. Greg has changed thousands of lives, human and canine, for the better. How many of us can say that?

Greg and Adella were gracious hosts when I stayed with them and Adella's son, Connor, at their Zanesville, Ohio, home. Rescue Road Trips is Adella's life too, and she shares Greg for half the year with all the dogs he brings north. It's not easy being apart half the time. Adella's love and support, not to mention her sandwiches, keep Greg rolling.

I first wrote about Greg for *Parade* magazine and I am grateful to Catherine DiBenedetto for embracing the story and helping me bring it to life. As soon as the article appeared in print, my wife, Judy, started pushing me to try and turn it into a book. She saw the potential before I did and wasn't going to stop leaning on me until I agreed to write the book proposal. She was right, and I am so thankful for her love, support, relentless prodding, and good judgment.

As soon as I mentioned the possibility of writing Greg's story to my agent Joelle Del-Bourgo, her only question was: How fast can you get a proposal to me? She, too, immediately saw the promise in this story. I've worked with Joelle on five books now and I am fortunate to have her as my advocate.

Stephanie Bowen, my astute and attentive editor at Sourcebooks, showed great enthusiasm for this project from the start. Thank you, Stephanie, for embracing *Rescue Road* and making it the best it could be. Also, my thanks to:

Liz Kelsch and Lathea Williams, my publicity team at Sourcebooks; Grace Menary-Winefield, the project editor; Becca Sage, the production editor; Adrienne Krogh in Sourcebooks' design department for her terrific work on a powerful and heartwarming cover; Jillian Rahn for her work on the internal design; and the many others who touched this book during the publication process, including Shana Drehs.

One person who had no say about spending many, many hours with me on the road was "Tommy," Greg's other driver and helping hand on the road. He was clear from the start he didn't want his real name used, but he puts in long hours helping Greg get these dogs to freedom, and though we had some good-natured arguments about politics on the road, he was always gracious and welcoming to me. The cab of that truck is a small space for two — even smaller for three. Thank you, Tommy.

Then there are the rescuers you read about who showed me ropes, took me to the shelters, the Dumpsters, and the pounds, and gave me a firsthand, up-close, unvarnished look at the rescue world. I am deeply grateful to Keri Bullock Toth first and foremost (who was also our Labs4rescue adoption coordinator for Albie); Greta Jones and Sarah Kelly of the CenLa Alliance for Animals; April Reeves, formerly of Lafayette Animal Aid; Melinda and Gary Falgout and Carly Faughn of Lafayette Animal Aid; Jamie Clark, a volunteer at Saint Martin Parish Animal Services and now with Lafayette Animal Aid; Tom English of Texas City, a freelance rescuer; Kathy Wetmore of Houston Shaggy Dog Rescue; Kelle Davis and Alicia McCarty of Forgotten Dogs of the Fifth Ward in Houston; Sarah Manns of Companion Animal Outreach in San Leon, Texas; Cathy Mahle of Labs4rescue and the many Labs4rescue volunteers I spoke or corresponded with; and Bethany Hickey of Mutts4rescue.

Many thanks to Dr. Bari Haas, Micheal Mitchell, and the staff of the Haas Animal Hospital in Pineville, Louisiana, where Keri Toth works as a vet tech. They let me hang out for a few days and observe them at work, splitting their time between paying clients and caring for all the rescues Keri brings in.

Two shelter directors spoke with me at some length and allowed me to tour their facilities, Michelle Brignac of Saint Martin

Parish Animal Services and Virginia Lee of Lafayette Animal Control. I am grateful to them and to Henry Wimbley of Alexandria Animal Control, who also permitted me to tour his shelter with Sarah Kelly. Mauricio Zepeda, adoption and volunteer coordinator of Houston's BARC shelter, gave me a thorough tour of BARC with Kathy Wetmore and answered all my questions.

Thanks too to Greg's Angels, especially Keith and Diane Remaly of the Allenton Angels, Lynda Ingle and Lynn Watson of the Birmingham Angels, and Annette Woodcock of the Rocky Hill Angels.

I owe a great debt to Krista Lombardo for saving Albie's life and caring for him while he was confined in the Alexandria shelter for several months waiting for someone — us it turned out — to give him his forever home. And I owe the same debt to CJ Nash for thinking fast and saving Salina and her littermates. CJ is a terrific young man, smart, worldly, and ambitious, with a future as wide as the horizon. It was a pleasure to meet him, his mother, and his brothers and to see where Salina was born.

I am so thankful to Rae McManus who helped save Salina, connected me with CJ and the Nash family, and became a terrific advocate for this book. Thank you, Rae and

Meredith, Rae's daughter.

Thank you to Tilani Pomirko who fostered Willis and poured her heart out in an interview shortly before Willis left for his forever home.

Jane Zippilli is an excellent photographer who chronicles many Gotcha Days in Spring Valley, New York. I am grateful to her for allowing us to use several of her images in this book. Thanks, too, to Alicia McCarty, Denise Trapani, and Larry Crawford for the use of their photos, as well.

Several adopting families allowed me to visit with them or spoke to me after their Gotcha Days so I could see how things were going. Thanks to Mary Ellen and Phil Gambutti, Glenna and Bill Mooney, Brenda Byers-Britney, Diana Ducharme and Luke and Tara McInerney, Jim Doyle, Anna Wright, the Dooley family, and Elizabeth Frampton.

To everyone who spoke with me for this book but whom I failed to mention by name, please forgive me for the oversight and *thank you.*

Finally, a shout-out to Café Medley on Sullivan's Island, South Carolina. For the price of a few cups of coffee, I rented a table in March of 2014 and wrote the book proposal for *Rescue Road.* A year later, I was back at the same table, revising the manuscript. It really is a special place where everyone knows your name.

PHOTO CREDITS

Page 10: Rescue Road Trips
Page 28: Peter Zheutlin
Page 65: Jane Zippilli
Page 103: Peter Zheutlin
Page 122: Jane Zippilli
Page 178: Peter Zheutlin
Page 201: Peter Zheutlin
Page 238: Forgotten Dogs of the Fifth Ward
   Project/Alicia McCarty
Page 258: Rescue Road Trips
Page 285: Rescue Road Trips
Page 315: Larry Crawford
Page 316: Rescue Road Trips
Page 340: Jane Zippilli
Page 359: Judy Gelman
Page 387: Judy Gelman

ABOUT THE AUTHOR

Peter Zheutlin is a freelance journalist and author whose work has appeared regularly in the *Boston Globe* and the *Christian Science Monitor.* Mr. Zheutlin has also written for the *Los Angeles Times, Parade* magazine, *AARP The Magazine,* and numerous other publications in the U.S. and abroad. He is the author of *Around the World on Two Wheels: Annie Londonderry's Extraordinary Ride* (Citadel Press, 2007). He is also the coauthor, with Thomas B. Graboys, MD, of *Life in the Balance: A Physician's Memoir of Life, Love, and Loss with Parkinson's Disease and Dementia* (Union Square Press, 2008), with Robert P. Smith, of *Riches Among the Ruins: Adventures in the Dark Corners of the Global Economy* (Amacom, 2009), and with Judith Gelman, of *The Unofficial Mad Men Cookbook: Inside the Kitchens, Bars, and Restaurants of* Mad Men (SmartPop/BenBella Books, 2011) and *The Unofficial Girls Guide to New York: Inside the Cafes, Clubs, and Neighborhoods of HBO's* Girls (SmartPop/BenBella, 2013). He resides in Massachusetts with his wife, author Judith Gelman, and has two grown sons. Visit him online at www.peterzheutlin.com.